Flying Safely

NEW, REVISED, AND ENLARGED EDITION

FLYING SAFELY

Richard L. Collins

DELACORTE PRESS / ELEANOR FRIEDE

Published by
Delacorte Press/Eleanor Friede
1 Dag Hammarskjold Plaza
New York, N.Y. 10017

Manufactured in the United States of America
First printing

LIBRARY OF CONGRESS CATALOGING IN PUBLICATION DATA

Collins, Richard L   1933–
    Flying safely.

    Includes index.
    1. Aeronautics—Safety measures.   2. Aeronautics—
Accidents.   I. Title.
TL553.5.C54   1980   629.132'5'0289   80-19383
ISBN 0-440-02652-0

To my father, Leighton Collins, in appreciation for the generous footsteps he has provided for me.

Contents

Foreword

The general aviation safety picture changes with time, and this revised edition of *Flying Safely* adds much new material to the original work. Here is the latest information from the National Transportation Safety Board and the FAA, including tables and graphs which show the comparative accident rates of contemporary as well as old airplanes. The lessons of more recent history are used to illustrate the nature of aviation: not inherently dangerous but very unforgiving of carelessness or neglect.

It is often tempting to list all accidents under the heading "pilot error," yet this is an oversimplification. Pilots do not fail on purpose. In the real world, pilots fail because they try to extract more utility or performance from an airplane than is available—or than is in proportion to their level skill.

Fear, the thing that protects us in many other situations,

often makes its suggestion too late in an airplane. Many a pilot has flown the last mile concerned not with aeronautical risk, but with thoughts of being late or missing an appointment. Flying safely must thus become second nature, a first-priority part of the action. The only way to accomplish this is through understanding.

That is the purpose of this book: to help you understand the things that lead to accidents. The tables and graphs that have been added are especially helpful in illustrating the strong correlation between the nature of specific airplanes and the ways in which pilots destroy them in accidents.

Some graphs in this book are based on National Transportation Safety Board studies and statistics. These are identified and need no explanation other than the accompanying text.

The tables compiled by the author are based on an unofficial survey of NTSB accident reports. They are not computer-generated since a personal examination of the brief-format accident reports often yields insight that is more useful in properly classifying an accident. The purpose of these tables (such as Figure 1 on page 21) is to detail accident types within a broader grouping, such as continuing VFR into adverse weather. The bars in these tables are formed by the actual aircraft involved in the accidents during the subject period. Aircraft are represented by a four-digit identification, in alphabetical order from the top. A key to the identifiers concludes this introduction.

Aircraft are not in the fleet in equal numbers so these tables must be considered with a grain of salt, or at least with some information on fleet size. The fleet size is indicated in the following key to identifiers. In parentheses, after the identification of each designation, the number of the particular aircraft registered with the FAA as of December, 1977 is included. The accident reports for 1975, 1976, 1977 and/or 1978 were the basis for most of the tables, so this census date represents a mid-period. I would add that the FAA's aircraft registry process appears to be approximate at best, and where aircraft are in the fleet in small numbers it would hardly be accurate to attempt the development of any true accident rate from this information. Flying hours vary, too. For example, there is no question that the 1,464 Debonairs and straight-tail Bonanzas fly far more hours annually than the 2,257 Ercoupes still registered. Hence no useful exposure-per-hour could be gained when comparing apple airplanes with orange airplanes. However, it is probable that similar airplanes fly similar amounts of hours annually so, as an example, the relative number of Bonanzas and Cessna 210's in a specific type accident would have specific meaning.

Helicopter, sailplane, and agricultural aircraft accidents are not included. In some instances, the accidents of one year were used to create a table; in others, two or three years were used. The variation is to make certain the sample is of meaningful size. The author has been compiling such information for more than twenty years and where one sample year appeared to offer an exception to past history, it was carefully checked to make certain it represented a real change and not a fluke. In most cases, only fatal accidents are considered.

The graphs based on NTSB studies contain information that the Board apparently felt to be valid. The tables that I generated are primarily to show what type airplanes were involved in what type accidents. In most of the tables, twins and singles have a separate column, to help the reader better evaluate the risks peculiar to each. The graphs are as accurate as possible, based on the nature of the information, and are for educational purposes only. They do not in any way reflect on the ability or capacity of any person, living or dead, or upon any aircraft or accessory intact or in little pieces.

Some airplanes are clustered under one type certificate by the manufacturer and, using NTSB information, it is often impossible to separate these airplanes. For example, the PA-28 covers all four-place Cherokees including the retractable Arrow, and the PA-32 covers the Cherokee 6, Lance and Saratoga series.

Designator	Description or Popular Name (Number in U.S. register)
A500	Aero Commander piston twins,
A520	includes Rockwell Shrike (957)
A560	
A680	
AA1A	Yankee, Grumman American TR-2 and Trainer (2,293)
AA5A	Grumman American Traveler, Cheetah and Tiger
AA5B	(167—this number an apparent error on the low side)
ARC3	Aeronca C-3, from the 1930's (49)

(All B and BE prefixes are from Beech Aircraft Corp.)

B100	King Air turboprops (1,107)
B200	
BE90	
BE18	Twin Beech (1,095)
BE19	Sport

BE23	Musketeer/Sundowner and
BE24	Musketeer Super R/Sierra (2,456)
BE33	Debonair/Bonanza (1,464)
BE35	V-tail Bonanza (6,810)
BE36	Stretched Bonanza (858)
BE45	Civil version of T-34 Trainer
BE50	Twin Bonanza (370)
BE55	Baron and
BE58	Stretched Baron (2,751)
BE60	Duke (296)
BE65	Queen Air (426)
BE76	Duchess (no meaningful number, date of census)
BE77	Skipper (no meaningful number, date of census)
BE95	Travel Air (500)
BGLE	Beagle 206 light twin from England (27)

(*All BL prefixes are Bellanca*)

BL7A	Bellanca singles, all taildraggers, including Citabria,
BL7D	Scout, Decathlon and Champion. Also includes
BL7E	Aeronca production of 7AC (4,822)
BL7G	
BL8G	
BL8K	
BL14	Four-place single, retractable, mostly Vikings (1,922)

(*All C prefixes are from Cessna Aircraft Company*)

C120	Two-place singles, mostly built in the late
C140	1940's (3,442)
C150	Known as such (16,504)
C152	
C170	Four-place taildragger, mostly 1950's (2,588)
C172	The ubiquitous Skyhawk (19,615)
C175	Skyhawk with 175 hp engine (1,431)
C177	Cardinals, including RG (2,853)
C180	Taildragger (2,573)
C182	Skylane (10,918)
C185	Taildragger (1,105)

C190	Big radial-engine singles, mostly late 1940's (589)
C195	
C205	Six-place singles, including Stationair 6 (2,320)
C206	
C207	Stationair 7 and Stationair 8 (199)
C210	Four- and six-place retractables, including turbocharged and pressurized Centurions (3,975)
C305	Civil version of L-19 "Bird Dog" (205)
C310	Light twins, known by number (3,370)
C320	
C336	Skymaster, push-pull twins, 337 is retractable (1,295)
C337	
C340	Pressurized light twin (468)
C401	Cabin-class unpressurized twins (1,305)
C402	
C404	
C411	
C414	Pressurized corporate piston twins, including
C421	Chancellor and Golden Eagle (913)
C441	Conquest (no meaningful number, date of census)
C500	Citation (253)
CVAR	Convair 240/340/440, ex-airliner (118)
DC3X	DC-3, Gooney Bird (596)
DHC2	De Havilland of Canada Beaver (333)
DHC3	De Havilland of Canada Otter (27)
DHC6	De Havilland of Canada Twin Otter (119)
ERCO	Ercoupe (2,257)
GLKS	Great Lakes Biplane (131)
HBLT	Homebuilt (8,660)
LJ23	Gates
LJ24	Learjets (511)
LJ25	

LJ35
LJ36

LLA4 Lake Buccaneer, amphibian (231)

LUS8 Luscombe two-place (2,279)

MAU4 Maule, four-place taildragger (418)

MO20 Mooney, all four-place (4,735)
MO22 Mooney Mustang, pressurized single (21)

MTU2 Mitsubishi MU-2, twin turboprop (350)

NAVN Navion (1,285)

P51D A real Mustang (142)

(*All* PA *prefixes are from Piper Aircraft Corporation*)

PAJ3 The original Cub (3,778)
PA11 A somewhat newer Cub (434)
PA12 Super Cruiser (1,361)
PA14 Family Cruiser (109)
PA15 Vagabond (306)
PA16 Clipper (394)
PA18 Super Cub (3,132)
PA20 Pacer (486)
PA22 Tri-Pacer (5,206)
PA23 Apache and Aztec (3,589)
PA24 Comanche, 180 hp through 400 hp (3,374)
PA28 Cherokee, 140 through 235, including retractable
    Arrow (17,968)
PA30 Twin Comanche (1,242)
PA31 Navajo (1,265)
PA32 Cherokee 6, Lance and Saratoga (2,767)
PA34 Seneca I and II (855)
PA38 Tomahawk (no meaningful number, date of census)
PA39 Twin Comanche CR (72)
PA44 Seminole (no meaningful number, date of census)

PAYE   Cheyenne turboprop (110)

PFLD   Porterfield, two-place from the 1930's (46)

PS2A   Pitts Special (101)

PT17   Stearman, biplane (482)

            (R *prefixes are from Rockwell International*)

R100   Fixed-gear single, formerly Volaire (362)
R112   200 hp retractable and
R114   260 hp retractable (520)
R200   Retractable, formerly Meyers (32)
R681   Turboprop twins (345)
R690
RSBL   Sabreliner business jet (268)

RYAN   Two-place, World War II trainer (168)

S226   Swearingen Merlin (148)

STNS   Stinson four-place, mostly from late 1940's (2,214)

SWFT   Globe/TEMCO Swift (680)

T600   Ted Smith and Piper Aerostars (346)
T601

TCFT   Taylorcraft, two-place (2,382)

V215   Varga 2150, two-place tandem (69)

WACO   Four-place retractable, import from Italy (55)

Even though there are only fifteen airplanes listed that I have not flown, the total number came as somewhat of a surprise. Reading over the list is enjoyable, too, and one thing stands out while reminiscing a bit about each machine:

There is not one that I would not like to fly again. Airplanes are like people. There is something to love in every one of them. And if the pilot does his part, any airplane can be flown with minimum risk. Read on; learn what to avoid in order to fly as safely as possible.

RICHARD L. COLLINS

1 | VFR Weather-Related Accidents

Gravity might be the most basic natural foe of the airplane, but weather is the most persistent victor over the airplane as pilots challenge nature with their mechanical birds. This is true regardless of the machine's sophistication or the pilot's level of skill. When air carriers have spectacular accidents, they almost always happen in bad weather. In fact, all the airlines would have a virtually perfect safety record if they flew only on clear days; they would also have no business after a few months of such an operation. This tells us that the risk in flying must increase as the ceiling and visibility decrease. This is the first and perhaps the most important thing a pilot must understand when starting to balance safety and utility in general aviation airplanes. The challenge is to fly as much weather as possible while at the same time minimizing the risk. This book's coverage of weather is directly related only to accident causes. The nature of weather and how to interpret it is another subject.

THE TYPICAL ACCIDENT

A pilot has to crawl before walking, and VFR flying might be characterized as the crawling phase. There is no way to get places very rapidly in VFR conditions unless the weather is excellent or unless you take a lot of chances. The risk of an accident increases as the square of chances taken, so a pilot who runs scud VFR, taking several chances a minute, is enjoying the highest-risk form of weather flying. The results are predictable, so predictable that the National Transportation Safety Board (NTSB) was able to publish a report that outlined a "typical" accident. The pilot had a private certificate, between 100 and 300 hours, and crashed in rain and fog. The pilot continued VFR into adverse weather conditions on a flight being conducted for pleasure or personal transportation. This "typical" accident is a prime safety problem in general aviation.

Things haven't changed much in years, because the first weather-related accident that I remember occurred twenty-eight years ago and fit the current average. This happened in the early fifties, when aviation wasn't nearly as formal as it is today. Instrument flying was not widely done, and many of those who flew weather did so through a combination of clandestine instrument flying and scud running. Most of this was self-taught, and the pilot with an Ercoupe in our hangar appeared serious about educating himself on weather flying. He outfitted the airplane with a manually rotatable loop for the low-frequency radio and added primary instruments, a turn-and-bank and vertical speed, to his panel. He talked quite a bit about the radio-navigation and instrument-flying ability he was developing, but I suppose the rest of us didn't pay much attention.

One rainy morning when we came to work at the airport, the Ercoupe was gone. It didn't return that evening, and the pilot's family became alarmed. We paid attention then. Nobody seemed to know where he had gone, and a check of his acquaintances in other communities yielded no clue. The weather improved the next day, and a search was launched.

Late in the afternoon, word came that the airplane had been spotted. A group of us were on the ground at the time and drove to join the party that was going to the site, about forty miles from the airport. We got there after dark, as they were removing the pilot from his shattered Ercoupe. It was an impressive sight. I had been flying for a couple of years, but until that instant I don't suppose I was completely convinced that airplanes could bite.

We went back the next day to watch the investigation. Most of the airplane was in one spot, but some fabric and parts from one wing were strewn through the woods in the direction from which the airplane came as the flight terminated. A nearby witness said a small airplane had flown over low and that one wing appeared to be "flapping."

The events leading to the accident started fitting into place. He crashed near a river bottom, and all of us knew from experience that the ceiling and visibility over the bottom land was always lower than elsewhere. General

conditions at reporting stations the morning of the accident
had been around 500 overcast with two miles visibility in
rain and fog. Clouds were probably in the treetops as the
pilot flew into this area. What next? The pilot apparently
pulled up, into the clouds. Nobody knows for sure what his
plan was, but perhaps he intended to fly instruments for a
while and then attempt a letdown. At this stage, the risk
involved probably wasn't apparent, and the pilot probably
was not frightened. In fact, he could have had a rather
methodical plan in mind for pressing on. But his self-taught
ability to fly instruments was not adequate. Control was
eventually lost, and the airplane was overstressed, resulting
in the failure of a wing. It was a classic case of a pilot
continuing VFR into adverse weather conditions and losing
control.

THE NEED TO "BE THERE" ON TIME

The pilot's mistake in continuing on into poor weather,
instead of retreating, is as typical today as it was in the
fifties. This part of the sequence leading to a weather-
related accident might be called the first stage.

To begin, why press on VFR, into the shadow of cloud
and possible disaster? The search for utility is a leading
reason. In this incident the pilot wanted to make the
Ercoupe work for him, to take him to a destination on
schedule even though the weather was not good. There is
probably an urgent compulsion to be somewhere behind
virtually all weather-related accidents. Whether it be a need

to get back home Sunday night for work on Monday, to "be there" for a big business deal, to get to a football game, to arrive on time for a clandestine meeting with a lover, or whatever, there's pride in being on time and at least imagined loss of face in canceling.

One key to risk management is to forget any attempt at scheduling arrivals on a VFR basis; weather is too fickle for a VFR pilot to say he's going to arrive anywhere at 8 A.M. next Tuesday. Another key is a continuing reevaluation of reasons for continuing once en route. If the continuation is related to business or pleasure, instead of the view ahead, the pilot has completely moved from the risk-management business to a reliance on luck, a very unreliable aeronautical commodity. It is often difficult to do, but the airplane and its environment must be mentally separated from all other considerations. There's just no way to allow the importance of a trip to influence the go/no-go decision without inviting trouble.

TRAINING

There are certainly considerations other than pressure to "be there" involved in VFR weather-related accidents. The training system has made a strong contribution to weather accidents by steadfastly refusing, over the years, to recognize the need for dual cross-country in marginal weather conditions. A lot of newly licensed private pilots probably fly on into instrument conditions simply because they do not know the visual appearance of the impossible. There is no way to learn the hazards of poking around in scud without doing it. Purists say that a pilot without instrument training should stay away from all clouds, that those who get close to clouds are breaking the law, and that this simple solution solves the total problem. True, in an idealistic sense, but every pilot is going to take a bite of the apple, and every pilot should thus be aware of the things that might bite back.

Being able to sample is one great advantage the airplane has over the automobile. An instructor can fly into marginal weather, get ice on the wings, shut engines off, stall, spin, and do all manner of terrible things with student pilots to show them the flaky side of the business. And these can all be done safely in carefully selected conditions. When I first taught our daughter to drive, I was a little taken by the fact that I couldn't demonstrate a blowout, a skid, or any of the bad things that happen in cars without donating one car to each demonstration. The hazards of marginal VFR can be safely demonstrated to students and they should be demonstrated. A school that gives dual cross-country only on clear days is simply not giving new pilots the tools necessary to make educated decisions on when to continue and when not to continue.

WEATHER INFORMATION

Weather information, and the way pilots consider it, is another integral part of the initial phase of continuing VFR into weather trouble. The time-honored system of checking the forecasts and the sequences is socially acceptable but rather ineffective. A good example of the hazards of such a procedure is found in western Arkansas and eastern Oklahoma. There is a notorious mountain there, Rich Mountain, that has been assaulted by a virtual squadron of airline, military, and general aviation aircraft over the years. (They haven't all actually hit Rich Mountain; some have used other mountains in the area.) The nearest airport weather-reporting stations are Fort Smith, Hot Springs, and Texarkana in Arkansas and McAlester, Oklahoma. It is quite common for all these stations to report good VFR and for Rich Mountain and its compatriots to be in the clouds. Many don't realize the hills are high in the area, and many pilots thus fly complacently (aided by a vortac on top of the mountain) into the area when the weather is bad and the ridges are obscured.

The FAA and the National Weather Service worked out a plan to put an automatic weather station atop Rich Mountain; this should help spread the word when the ridges are obscured. There is no way to put an automatic station on every hill and in every river bottom area, though, so pilots will forever be left to interpret and interpolate. The hazard comes when a pilot sets out with a determination that the weather is going to be okay—wearing rose-colored glasses, if you will—and presses on with the thought that the reported weather behind is good, the reported weather to one side is good, the reported weather at a station up ahead is good, and the forecasts are good, so it's bound to be okay to fly on regardless of how bad it looks through the windshield. Visual is VFR's first name, so what the pilot sees just has to be assigned a lot of weight in the decision process.

HELP FROM BELOW

Another contributing factor, a rather insidious one, is the feeling some pilots have that people on the ground can truly help an airplane in flight. This concept suggests that it might be okay to fly on until belly button deep in alligators and then call and transfer the mess to Big Brother. There are some situations in which a person on the ground can give meaningful help to a pilot in distress by giving location or soothing advice, but fate is squarely in the pilot's hand a great majority of the time.

It is interesting to contemplate that back in the good old days before radio, pilots made a lot of precautionary cow-pasture landings in bad weather. This was that day's form of going for help after pressing on too far, and it worked rather well. Now the airplanes don't do so well in pastures, so perhaps the feeling has changed to one of calling for help, calling the FAA as an "out," except that this modern version of going for help often doesn't work. The pilots of the good old days could, for a fact, extricate themselves with the precautionary landing because in so doing they satisfied the basic responsibility of flying the airplane until it stopped. Picking up a microphone does not satisfy that basic responsibility.

BLUE SHIELD

Another factor contributing to modern-day complacency is the smattering of instrument training given to student pilots. This could lead a person to believe that "I can handle it" after flying inadvertently into cloud. Some perhaps can, especially if they work at maintaining proficiency, but many private pilots lose instrument proficiency and find themselves unable to fly instruments when the chips are down. Another fact argues strongly against the value of limited instrument training. Every year there are a substantial number of "continued VFR" accidents in which the pilot actually has an instrument rating. How can you explain an instrument pilot breaking an airplane trying to fly VFR in marginal weather? For one thing, the hardness of rock is unimpressed by FAA ratings. Also, there are instances of loss of control—inability to fly on the gauges—by instrument pilots. Perhaps they just can't perform when suddenly thrust into IFR conditions. The key to VFR is staying VFR regardless of the words on your license.

One of the prime things we learn when combining and considering the factors in the first stage of a VFR weather-related accident is that the pilot must learn to isolate flying from other things and fly only on the basis of aeronautical right and wrong. If the flight is continued on the basis of business or pleasure, if clouds are viewed through rose-colored glasses, and/or if the pilot flies into a mess feeling

secure because of available help from the ground or minimum instrument instruction in basic flight training, then
conditions are set for the second stage.

SECOND STAGE

Discussion of the first stage is related to thought processes.
There's some of that in the second stage, too, but there are
also statistics to use in drawing a picture of what happens in
VFR weather-related accidents. For example, we know that
the bulk of the accidents occur en route, when pilots either
fly into the ground still in control of the aircraft or when
they hit the ground riding as a passenger, having lost control of the aircraft.

Figure 1 shows the distribution of fatal VFR weather-
related accidents among three causes. Twins and singles are
separated. This represents a one-year period. It is quite
plain that flying into the ground in control, and losing control and then hitting the ground, appear to be equally popu-
lar. However, if the airframe failures in flight are added to
the "out of control" column, then that type accident accounts for a major part of the problem. This is where the
airframe failures belong, too. No question—when there's
an airframe failure without a relationship of thunderstorm
turbulence, the pilot loses control of the airplane. Most
thunderstorm accidents involve a loss of control, too, and
we'll discuss that later.

(When using the figures in this book, remember that
there is no allowance made for the number of each type

TWINS	SINGLES	TWINS	SINGLES	TWINS	SINGLES
	AA5A		AA5A		
	AA5B		AA5A		
	AA5B		BE24		
	BE33		BE33		
	BE35		BE35		
	BE35		BE35		
	BL14		BL14		
	BL14		C150		
	BL14		C150		
	C150		C150		
	C152		C170		
	C152		C172		
	C172		C172		
	C172		C172		
	C172		C172		
	C172		C172		
	C172		C172		
	C172		C172		
	C172		C172		
	C172		C172		
	C177		C177		
	C180		C177		
	C180		C182		
	C182		C182		
	C182		C182		
	C182		C182		
	C182		C185		
	C185		C206		
	C206		MO20		
	C206		MO20		
	C206		NAVN		
	C210		PA18		
	C210		PA18		
	MO20		PA24		
	MO20		PA24		
	MO20		PA28		
	MO20		PA28		
	PA28		PA28		
	PA28		PA28		
	PA28		PA28		BE35
	PA28		PA28		BE35
A680	PA28		PA28		BE35
BE50	PA28		PA28		PA24
BE55	PA28		PA28		PA24
C310	PA28		PA28		PA28
C320	PA28		PA28		PA28
C340	PA28		PA28		PA28
C411	PA32		PA28		PA28
PA23	PA32	BE55	PA28		PA32
PA23	PA32	C310	PA28	No	PA32
PA31	STNS	PA30	PA32	Twin	PA32

TWINS	SINGLES	TWINS	SINGLES	TWINS	SINGLES
Flew into ground, in control		**Hit ground, out of control**		**Airframe failure, no thunderstorm**	

Figure 1. VFR flight, fatal weather-related accidents. One year.

aircraft in the fleet, or for hours flown, unless so stated. This table and the others like it that follow, show only the loss experience in a recent period. They should be used to see which classes of airplanes seem more prone to a particular type accident. Be advised that some airplane type certificates cover a number of airplanes. A PA-28 might be a Cherokee 140, 150, 160, 180 or 235, or it might be a retractable Arrow, for example. A PA-32 could be a 6, Lance or Saratoga. A 177 could be a Cardinal or a Cardinal RG. See pages 4–8 for a complete explanation of the table symbols.)

In Figure 1 we see that the pilots of twins are far less likely to have a weather accident involving loss of control than are the pilots of singles. More training is probably one reason. The higher likelihood of having a good autopilot could be another reason. In singles, there doesn't appear to be any great predominance of retractables in either of the tall columns. In fact, this appears to be a cross-section of the general aviation fleet, with some emphasis on basic four-place airplanes. I ascertained from the accident reports that most of the PA-28's and PA-32's in the airframe failure column are Arrows or Lances, so retractables account for virtually all the involvement here. I've been following this subject for years, and this has always been the case.

IN CONTROL

VFR weather-related accidents in which the pilot flies into high terrain can happen for several reasons. A well-documented example of simply flying into a mountain came several years ago when a Texas International Airlines Convair continued VFR into adverse weather and did the deed. It was night, as is so often the case in VFR weather accidents. The crew of the airliner was trying to circumnavigate a line of storms while flying VFR, using airborne weather radar for information on the storms. On the short 62-nautical-mile hop from El Dorado to Texarkana, Arkansas, the crew deviated about 100 nautical miles north of course where it met with disaster. The cockpit voice recorder tape from the accident gives all pilots a unique opportunity to contemplate the actions leading to such an accident. In the transcript, the pilots were talking to one another. In a similar situation, a general aviation pilot might be talking to himself, or just thinking. The transcript covers about the last ten minutes of conversation in the cockpit. It's give and take between the Captain and the First Officer.

"Yeah, I'd stay down. You're right in the . . . right in the base of the clouds. . . . I tell you what, we're going to be able to turn here in a minute."

"You wanna go through there?"

"Yeah."

"All right. . . . Good, looking good, Mac. Looking good."

"That's all right, wait a minute."

"Well, I can't even get, ah, Texarkana anymore."

"I'll tell you what, Fred . . ."

" 'kay boss."

"Well, ah, we'll just try that, we'll try it. We're gonna be in the rain pretty soon. It's only about two miles wide."

"You tell me where you want me to go."

"Okay, give me a heading of, ah, three forty."

"Three forty?"

"Three forty . . . steady on. . . . We got ten miles to go 'n'
. . . we're gonna turn. . . . To the left, ah, 'bout fifty degrees."

"Want me to turn, did ya say fifty?"

"Yeah, fifty left. . . . On about, uh, two ninety."

"Two ninety."

"You got six miles to turn . . . three miles south of turn."

"We're in it."

"Huh?"

"We're in solid, now."

"Are we?"

"Hold it."

"Start your turn. Standard rate. . . . Level out and let me
see it when you hit two ninety."

"Aw, okay. . . . There's your two ninety."

"Steady on . . . should hit in about a half a mile. Should
be out of it in 'bout two miles. . . . You're in it. . . . Are you
through it? . . . Turn thirty left."

"I can see the ground now. . . . There's thirty left, naw,
that's thirty-five."

"Keep on truckin', just keep on a-truckin'."

"Well, we must be somewhere in Oklahoma."

"Doin' all the good in the world."

"Do you have any idea of what the frequency of the
Paris VOR is?"

"Nope, don't really give a #@. . . . Put, uh, about two
sixty-five, heading two sixty-five."

"Heading two sixty-five. . . . I would say we # up."

"Think so (*laughter*) . . . Didn't we? . . . Fred, descend
to two thousand."

"Two thousand, coming down. . . . Here we are, we're not out of it."

"Let's truck on . . . 'bout five to the right. . . . Shift over a little bit if you can. . . . Sure can. . . . That's all right."

"Right, #"

"That's all right, you're doing all the good in the world. . . . I thought we'd get . . . I thought it was moving that way on me only. We just kinda turned a little bit while you was looking at the map."

"Look."

"First time I ever made a mistake in my life."

"I'll be #. Man, I wish I knew where we were so we'd have some idea of the general # terrain around this # place."

"I know what it is."

"What?"

"That the highest point out here is about twelve hundred feet. . . . The whole general area, and then we're not even where that is, I don't believe."

"I'll tell you what, as long as we travel northwest instead of west, and I still can't get Paris."

(*Whistling.*)

"Go ahead and look at it."

(*Whistling.*)

"Two hundred and fifty, we're about to pass over Page VOR . . . you know where that is?"

"Yeah."

"All right."

"About a hundred and eighty degrees to Texarkana."

"About a hundred and fifty-two . . . minimum en route altitude here is forty-four hund . . ."

He was interrupted in mid-sentence by impact with the slope of Black Fork Mountain.

That is a rather dramatic demonstration of the fact that mountains are where you find them, not where you think they are. Many general aviation airplanes are lost in this manner every year, and special problems arise when pilots accustomed to flying in flat country tackle the mountains in adverse weather conditions. In fact, almost half the general aviation airplanes that become the subject of search-and-rescue missions are lost in mountainous terrain in marginal VFR conditions.

FLAT COUNTRY

Not all hit mountains, and a VFR pilot running the scud in flat country can fall victim to an erroneous old superstition that there's always a ceiling: Fly low enough and you can see. More than one pilot has entered IFR conditions and then started a descent to get below the clouds only to find the ceiling about halfway down the old oak tree. Another way people frequently fail is in trying to turn around in scud and cloud after things go sour on a railroad- or highway-following flight plan. Roads, rail and otherwise, often follow the lowest ground, so any turn might be toward higher ground. Also, if the airplane is only a couple of hundred feet off the deck, that much altitude is easy to lose in a turn. Losing 200 feet in a turn doesn't qualify as loss of control, but it can be disastrous in certain situations.

However it is done, most of the pilots who fly into the

ground in adverse weather do a complete job of wrapping things up. The airplane is almost always moving along at normal cruise, which is usually too fast for survival. There are exceptions, but the exceptions usually come when the airplane is being operated at speeds lower than normal cruise. One I know of involved flight into a hillside during a climb. The pilot just hit the hill without seeing it, but speed was low and the angle of impact was moderated by the airplane's climb angle. The occupants were hardly scratched. Shoulder-harness systems help a great deal in such situations.

LOSS OF CONTROL

When a VFR pilot enters adverse weather conditions and then loses control, one of two things happens: The airplane hangs together until it hits the ground or the airframe fails in flight. These two areas need to be statistically separated for basic discussion.

In the great majority of accidents, the airplane reaches the ground in one piece after the pilot loses control. In about 20 percent of the accidents, the pilot overstresses the airplane and at least some part of it fails before the airplane hits the ground. In either case, the cause is the same: The pilot lost control. The technical difference in outcome really has little bearing on the accident and is related more to the configuration of the aircraft than anything else. When a pilot loses control of an aerodynamically clean airplane, which certainly means it has retractable gear, the airspeed tends to build very rapidly unless the pilot extends the gear and closes the throttle. The airspeed moves into the yellow caution area and soon flirts with the red line. The airplane usually establishes itself in a spiral dive—a maneuver with high airspeed, steep angle of bank, and a steep nose-down attitude. The airplane probably doesn't break itself in the spiral dive, but at high airspeed it doesn't take much additional g-load to put tons more load on the structure than it was designed to stand. Breakup comes in a recovery attempt: Level the wings and pull out of the screaming dive. Or perhaps the pilot senses the "dive" more strongly than the "turn" and pulls the airplane apart in the spiral.

The theory has been advanced that the lighter the longitudinal control forces, the higher the incidence of airframe failure in flight. That theory might have some basis— statistics could be developed that would tend to bear it out —but the final outcome of the event might not be so different. Once a VFR pilot loses control on instruments, only a stroke of luck is likely to salvage the flight. And if you take the total of loss-of-control accidents, the various makes and models tend to come out about even. Some just specialize in breaking before they hit the ground rather than after. This will be covered fully in Chapter 8.

Thunderstorms play a role in some VFR weather-related airframe failures in flight. In some years I have studied, the number is high in relation to the non-thunderstorm airframe failures; in others it is low. In some years there have actually been more airframe failures in thunderstorms involving VFR than IFR aircraft. This is still more of an IFR subject, so it will be treated fully in Chapter 2. The VFR pilot who presses on and winds up inside a cloud is in a perilous state; make that cloud a cumulonimbus and there's not much left to discuss.

PRELIMINARIES

Regardless of what happens after a loss of control, the preliminaries probably have something in common. Disaster strikes when the pilot is diverted from the basic task of keeping the wings level. This might happen almost instantly, or it might take a while. At times, a noninstrument pilot gets off to a good start and manages for a considerable time on instruments, only to lose control because of a diversion. Perhaps a little turbulence is the straw, or it could be something simple like time taken to look at a map or fool with a radio. The sum of the accidents strongly suggests that a VFR pilot trying to fly gauges should concentrate on the basics for a while before doing anything else and should never stray very far from the basics. There might be a great compulsion to look at a chart, turn right, turn left, go up, go down, or use the radio, but in the final analysis the pilot is probably going to save himself with the ability to keep the airplane right side up. Settling in with that for a moment before fooling with anything else would have to be considered best in most situations.

Whereas the pilot who flies into the ground under control usually does so suddenly—soon after entering inclement weather or reaching high terrain—the pilot who flies into cloud, does not hit something, and survives the first

few minutes on instruments still has a chance. He gets to
make a few more mistakes, or to make up for past mistakes,
by doing it correctly. It is from these incidents that the
dramatic tape recordings of pilot-controller conversations
are developed—these are usually the unsuccessful events.
There are occasional successful saves—perhaps enough to
create the image that there is a life preserver hanging on the
clouds—but the bad outcomes outnumber the good. Real
success lies in staying out of the clouds when flying VFR.

PILOT UNDERSTANDING OF RISK

Weather-related accidents involving VFR pilots pose quite
a dilemma. A person who learns to fly can only be expected
to quickly develop the desire to put flying to practical use.
The next step is to start pushing the horizons back. Then
the time comes when there is adverse weather between the
pilot and an intended destination, and the fine line between
possible and impossible becomes the challenge and the
problem.

   To some, the problem is simple once the ingredients are
understood. The VFR pilot in adverse weather conditions is
breaking the law, doing something he was not trained to do,
and flying in a manner contrary to the advice of more
knowledgeable pilots. The government might try to treat
the problem by raising the VFR minimums, but that is a
questionable way to do it. New rules would be just as easy
to break as old ones. Also, VFR weather minimums are as
diffuse as cloud. Who really knows when an airplane is

2,000 feet horizontally from a cloud? I've never seen a tape measure that long. More training is another cure that is often advanced, and this would help if the training addressed the proper area—the nitty-gritty of interpreting weather in person.

Human nature being what it is, the best remedy is in pilot understanding of the risks involved. A small percentage of the flying is done by VFR pilots in adverse weather conditions, but a very high percentage of the serious general aviation accidents involve VFR pilots in adverse weather conditions. A pilot flying VFR without three miles visibility and without a ceiling that is at least 1,000 feet above the highest obstacle five miles either side of the proposed flight path is simply engaging in one of the most hazardous forms of flying. No question about it, that's not the way to fly weather.

2 | IFR Weather-Related Accidents

There is a substantial difference in the risk involved during marginal VFR and IFR flying. Scud running is an inexact aeronautical science where IFR is a precise form of flying. Too, relatively high risk is involved in only a small percentage of IFR flying time, where high risk is continuous in any marginal VFR operation.

There is a procedure and a number for most everything in IFR; the pilot's work is to match the numbers on the panel with the numbers on the chart. Marginal VFR involves numbers, too, but this is mixed with equal amounts of intuition and pure blind luck.

Marginal VFR is by far the more dangerous of the two forms of flying, but it isn't possible to put an exact value on the IFR advantage over marginal VFR. No figures are available for the hours flown in each category. We do know that about 30 percent of the fatal weather-related accidents in general aviation involve instrument-rated pilots flying on IFR flight plans, though, and we can use this as a basis for contemplating possible relative accident rates. If marginal VFR hours and IFR hours are equal, then the safety record for IFR is more than twice as good. The IFR record likely enjoys a much better advantage than that, though, because the IFR hours probably exceed marginal VFR hours by a wide margin. The figure might be twenty times if all the necessary ingredients were available for a true determination. I would add that as time runs, IFR accidents become a larger part of the weather-related accident picture. This is logical because more pilots have and use instrument ratings each year, where VFR cross-country flying probably doesn't increase much.

Less risk and greater utility is quite a combination. The IFR accident picture also suggests that the instrument-rated pilot can easily develop a guard against the most frequent accident causes.

Figure 2 covers fatal accidents that occurred in three full years' worth of IFR flying. I expanded the period from the one-year period used for VFR to get a good sample. Glance back at Figure 1 to get an example of the greater nature of our VFR problem. One year of VFR problems is about the size of three years of IFR problems. Here, all aircraft were on an IFR flight plan, were operated by a properly certificated pilot, and weather was a factor in each accident. In other words, if a blowout on takeoff caused an airplane on an IFR flight plan to career into a ditch, that accident isn't included.

Ice		Thunder, including airframe failure in thunderstorms		Descent and approach		Loss of control, not related to thunder		Mechanical, incl. radio and accessories but not engines		Airframe failure, not turbulence-related		Fuel exhaustion		Engine failure		Departure	
TWIN	SNGL	TWIN	SNGL	TWIN	SNGL	TWIN	SNGL	TWIN	SNGL	TWIN	SNGL	TWIN	SNGL	TWIN	SNGL	TWIN	SNGL
A560	BE35	BE18	BE35	A500	BE35	BE18	BE23	A680	BE35	PA30	BE35	C310	None	BE18	C206	BE18	C210
BE18	C150	C421	BE35	A560	BE36	BE50	BE33	C337	BE35	PA31	BE35	C337		BE55		BE50	PA28
BE50	C182	PA23	BE35	A680	C172	BE55	BE35	C411	C210	PA34	BE35	MTU2		BE58		BE55	PA32
BE55	C206	PA23	BE36	BE18	C172	BE55	BE36	PA23	C210		BE35	PA30		BE95		BE55	PA32
C310	C210	PA30	BL14	BE18	C177	BE58	C182	PA31	MO22		PA24			BE95		BE90	
C337	PA28	T600	C210	BE55	C177	BE90	C206		PA24		PA28			C320		PA23	
C411	V215		C210	BE58	C182	BE95	C210		PA24					C421		PA23	
C414			MO20	BE60	C182	BGLE	C210		PA28					MTU2		PA31	
PA23			PA28	BE90	C182	C310	MO20		R112					PA34			
PA34				BE90	C210	C310	PA24										
PA39				BE95	C210	C310	PA28										
				BE95	MO20	PA23	PA28										
				B100	MO20	PA23	PA28										
				B200	MO20	PA23											
				C320	MO20	PA34											
				C337	PA28	PAYE											
				C337	PA32												
				C340	R112												
				C402													
				LJ24													
				MTU2													
				PA23													
				PA34													
				PAYE													
				R690													
				RSBL													
				S226													
				S226													

Figure 2. IFR flight, fatal weather-related accidents. Three years.

THE CHILL FACTOR

Ice: we find that general aviation pilots show a healthy respect for the frosty stuff; it was a factor in only nineteen IFR accidents in the three-year period selected as an example. And it is heartening that you can study the circumstances in most ice-related accidents and imagine how the flight could have been flown to a successful, if not a routine, conclusion.

If a pilot has recurring nightmares about icing encounters, he's likely to dream the textbook horror story of tremendous ice accumulation in a few minutes. The airplane will become festooned with giant icicles and will finally crash to the ground because of the weight and deformity of the frozen decoration. A pretty good dream, but it seldom works that way. In the majority of ice-related accidents, the pilot stacks some other basic errors on top of the ice to create the impossible situation. This makes it important to look beyond the ice instead of shrugging and just saying that the ice did it.

One pilot crashed on approach in a well-iced airplane. It was the third approach to that airport, so the pilot must have wanted badly to land there. He persisted in the effort to land despite the ice, and it is entirely possible that the pilot would have descended into the ground without any ice on the airplane. In other words, the ice might have been incidental. This theme recurs in so-called icing accidents. As in this example, many low-level icing situations also involve low ceilings and fog, which in turn lead a pilot to take risks that might be unrelated to icing. The airplane crashes with ice adhering to it so that is listed as a factor. Perhaps it should just be listed as the last straw.

THE ICED AIRPLANES

In the three-year period covered by Figure 2, very few single-engine airplanes were equipped with de-icing equipment. This was just beginning to be made available for singles at the time. Yet twins, many of which were undoubtedly equipped with de-icing, outnumber singles in icing accidents by a good margin. Why might this be? I suspect that pilots flying singles are more attuned to the theory of alternative action in case of ice and are prone to flee the stuff at first frosting. Pilots flying twins might be taken by the big-iron syndrome: "I can fly through hell, or ice, in my airplane because it has two engines."

The risk involved in ice is hardly altered by the number of engines on an airplane. And even though a twin probably has better climb capability than a single going into an icing situation, the twin probably loses climb capability more quickly because it offers greater surface area for ice collection than does a single of comparable airframe size. This is true even with de-iced airplanes: Two engines and a big bare nose can collect ice in a hurry.

The twin's greater involvement in ice-related accidents doesn't mean it is safer to fly ice in a single—it does suggest, however, that single pilots do a better job of staying away from ice.

It's important to understand de-icing equipment. The boots on the wings and tail are actually de-icers. Ice is allowed to build, then tubes in the boots are inflated to break the ice. The slipstream blows it away. This sounds neat and clean, but it isn't. Cycle the boots with just a little ice and a lot of it won't blow away. Then new ice will build atop the old. Even if the boots are cycled at the proper time—after accumulation of from a quarter- to a half-inch of ice—the clean-up job isn't likely to be complete. The point: Boots are something to use while fleeing ice, not something to use in slogging through ice for hours. The accumulation you can get on an equipped airplane will slow it down, and in extreme cases will bring it to the ground.

For props and windshields, the most common form of ice protection is electric heat—elements encased in rubber handle the prop, and a plate or section of the windshield containing heating elements is used to clear enough area to see for landing. Prop and windshield equipment is considered as anti-ice—it is turned on in advance, to keep ice off.

Important: If an airplane has ice protection equipment and is not certified for flight into known icing conditions, it either does not have a complete array of gear, it has not been flight tested in ice, or it has been flight tested in ice and the equipment was found lacking. Such equipment should be used only to minimize the effect of ice when fleeing an icing situation. That's really what equipment on a certified airplane is used for, but there you at least know that the system has actually been tested in ice.

There were no turbine airplanes involved in icing accidents in this three-year period. All turbines have certified ice protection equipment, but their strong rates of climb and high operating altitudes probably have more to do with their lack of involvement in icing accidents than anything else.

WAR STORIES

It is interesting that even pilots with considerable IFR experience have relatively few really bad ice tales to tell. Perhaps this is because ice does develop slowly, giving time to plan. Most pilots start planning quickly and develop an alternate course of action that deals with the ice situation. Even in serious icing situations, fast action is usually rewarding so war stories are minimized.

I offer one ice tale—of a flight in a 250 Comanche. It was late December. The forecast had initially been for clear weather over the entire New York-to-Dallas route, but things were destined to become interesting. It was raining when we stopped in Nashville, and a careful rethink was in order.

Despite the fact the weather was worse than forecast, the briefer saw no problem in an IFR flight to the Southwest. Six thousand would be a good ice-free level, he said, so we launched with that altitude requested.

The weather decided to do its icy thing before we reached Memphis. The air became quite turbulent, and ice started building rapidly on the Comanche. The surface weather was having its problems, too, with ceilings and visibilities quite low in what was turning into a real snowstorm. The time had come for a fast decision, and there was no question in this case that the thing to do was land as soon as possible. There were a couple of small airports available with instrument approaches, but I chose Memphis because of its full instrument landing system. A missed approach would be a bad deal, and I was motivated to fly that ILS with some precision. It all worked well, but the airplane wouldn't have been good for many more miles had the ice continued to accumulate.

The elapsed time from the first collection of ice to landing was probably not over thirty minutes. The moral was that ice is bad, but it can be handled if something is done about it. That "something" would almost never be a continuation of the present status.

WATCH THE BASICS

Once ice appears and something is done to get away from it the record is clear in suggesting that the pilot pay careful attention to the aerodynamics of ice as well as to minimum altitudes and other staples. Many ice-related accidents end in a stall and spin, which comes about after the pilot has mastered everything but the final approach and landing. In one such event, the pilot collected a respectable but not debilitating amount of ice and then stalled while turning on final approach after making an instrument approach. The surface wind was strong and across the runway, and in setting up the circle for landing after breaking out of the clouds, the pilot had elected to circle to the left. By so doing, he subjected the airplane to a very strong downwind component on base leg. The additional groundspeed caused an overshoot of the turn onto final; the pilot probably steepened the bank to try to complete the turn, and zap, the airplane stalled and started to spin. The ice on the wings no doubt contributed to the accident, but it was far from the sole cause. The outcome might have been the same without the ice.

The weight and deformity of ice does increase the stalling speed of an airplane. Another thing it can do is foul up the airflow over the tail of an airplane when the flaps are extended. As a result, the use of flaps is not recommended when flying with ice on many or most airplanes. The pilot's operating handbook should have the word on this. Ice plus no flaps would call for careful calculation of proper approach speed. Some knots would need to be added for ice in addition to the extra speed required for a no-flap approach.

GEOGRAPHY

The geography of icing accidents is also interesting. The worst dream about ice calls for the airplane to be unable to maintain altitude in mountainous terrain, and while this does happen, most icing accidents happen in flat country. Perhaps this is an illustration that pilot fear of ice is multiplied in rough terrain, especially in the Rockies, and people are more careful about staying away from the stuff there.

Positional awareness and a knowledge of the terrain are

important ice-related items when flying in rough terrain. Knowledge of the ridge locations (and height) and the valley locations in relation to the position of the airplane can save the day. The snap judgment might be that the closest airport is the best one to head for, but if it is dark, there's no weather reporting at that airport and only a VOR approach, and there are ridges in the area, an ILS airport in a wide valley a few miles farther away might be by far the best deal.

The relatively small number of ice-related IFR accidents, and the fact that ice is not the sole cause in most instances, should not belittle the importance of the risk that comes with icing encounters. The risk is there, and it probably increases as the square of the time spent flying in icing conditions. The only answer to ice is to get out of it: Climb, descend, retreat, or land.

THUNDER

Thunderstorms appear in the IFR accident column with about the same frequency as ice; there were seventeen in the three-year period. The similarity ends there. Thunderstorms are an either/or situation: Either you are in one or you are not. Whereas a pilot's ice planning might reach a peak after ice has started to accumulate, a pilot's thunderstorm planning had best start before the airplane is in one of the beasts. There is a contrast in equipment involved in thunderstorm accidents, too. More of the thunderstorm aircraft were singles. Perhaps singles fly more IFR hours than twins and thus have greater exposure, but there should be more to it than that. It is an interesting place to start examining the thunderstorm question.

One prone to jump to conclusions might say that twins have less thunderstorm accidents because they are bigger and stronger. There could be some logic to that, but the thought is still misleading. The strength requirement for general aviation airplanes is built around two factors, g-loading and the consideration of a vertical gust of a given strength. The requirements are identical for all airplanes weighing under 6,000 pounds. Above 6,000 pounds, the g-loading requirement decreases, but the vertical gust that must be considered remains the same. This leaves the impression that all airplanes are equal in thunderstorm turbulence, regardless of size, wing loading, and speed. This is also misleading for several reasons.

THERE IS A DIFFERENCE

First and foremost, anyone who has ridden through a thunderstorm in a large airplane and in a small airplane knows that there is a difference. The difference is not related to brute strength—the certification rules handle that—it is more often related to controllability. When airframe failure in flight occurs in a thunderstorm-related accident, it is usually established that the failure occurred after the pilot lost control of the airplane, not as the airplane initially entered an area of turbulence. (This, incidentally, is relatively easy to establish by studying the nature and sequence of the airframe failure.)

What loss of control tells us is that while large and small airplanes might be more or less equal in ability to withstand turbulence, they are apparently far apart in their ability to be flown in turbulence. Or, the pilots who fly them are not equal in ability. There is probably substance to both thoughts.

A lighter airplane is likely to be slower and will thus spend more time in turbulence. The possibility of losing control would have to be in direct proportion to the time spent in turbulence. Displacements will also be greater than might be the case with larger, faster, or heavier aircraft. Pit a 40-foot-per-second gust against an airplane flying at 100 knots and against an airplane flying at 200 knots, and while the g-load might be the same, the upward displacement of the faster airplane would be much less—just as a forty-knot crosswind would have less effect on the ground track of the faster airplane. Consider it in another light. The angle-of-attack increases in response to the gust in the 100-knot airplane would be half as rapid and the airplane's response to the change would thus take twice as long. Faster airplanes might develop relatively high g-loads while flying through the same bit of turbulence as a light airplane, but the ride in the faster or heavier airplane is felt more as sharp jabs, annoyances that come and go rather quickly, whereas the slower airplane wallows and pitches much more.

When considering the controllability of larger versus smaller airplanes, we must also acknowledge that the smaller airplane is more affected simply because of size. As it flies slowly through shear, eddies, and gusts, a greater percentage of the whole machine can be in the influence of the small but violent disturbances at one time.

EXPERIENCE

People who fly a lot in thunderstorm country find that the beasts always tend to be different and that avoidance is the only real key to success. You might note a pilot flying through a bad-looking area without having a problem, and as you take a bite yourself there are times when the ferocity of a storm seems perhaps not so overwhelming. Then a rough experience changes all that.

I have a vivid recollection of one encounter. It was between Fort Smith and Little Rock, Arkansas. There was no radar in the airplane, and this was before the time of air route traffic control radar to help with weather avoidance. The briefing had suggested scattered thunderstorms, and the dark mass of sky ahead should have told me that they were scattered generously along my path. But that was no deterrent as I kept the nose of the rugged old Twin Bonanza pointed straight ahead.

The first sensation was of acceleration and g-load. The airspeed was increasing and the airplane was ascending; both were happening quite rapidly. Within the ascending air were staccato-sharp jabs. I've forgotten the amount of ascent, but it came to several thousand feet, even with the engines throttled back. I was concerned about not maintaining altitude but said nothing to the FAA controller (then CAA) about it. The microphone had fallen off its hook, and I felt that my time had best be devoted to taming the airplane. I also thought that any other airplane in there would also have been ascending.

I did consider turning around but hesitated because my ability was being sorely taxed by the straight-and-level chore. I think it was a good decision, too, because in studying accident reports I have found quite a number in which it appears almost certain that the pilot lost control as a turn was attempted after a storm had been penetrated. The best time to turn is before entering a storm. Also, it is often noted that when an airplane crashes in a thunderstorm area, the witnesses report that the heavy rain started after the crash. This suggests that the worst turbulence might be found around the edges of the heavy precipitation, not in it, not once you have flown past the teeth of the storm and into its gullet. Weather research tends to support this theory, so presumably I did the right thing by continuing after making the initial mistake.

AERIAL SUBMARINE

After the updraft came the heavy, the unbelievably heavy, rain. It was like being in a submarine. The eroding effect of the water took all the paint off the leading edges of the almost new airplane. The turbulence remained in the rain, but it did not seem as bad as before the water was reached. The serious bumps did resume as I flew back out of the rain area, and, in retrospect, the greatest difficulty in the turbulence came from not being able to see the instruments clearly. The Twin Bonanza had a soft seat, and the panel became a jumbled blur as I bounced up and down. The airplane did have one of those big, old-fashioned, surplus World War II artificial horizons; it was the easiest thing to see so I finally just concentrated on it and nothing else.

Flying an approximate heading was not as much a problem as altitude control, but I could see where roll control would become quite a consideration in an airplane with less powerful lateral control than the Twin Bonanza.

So it can work. If avoidance fails, if the big mistake is made, it doesn't automatically mean total failure. The relatively low number of thunderstorm-related IFR accidents bears this out. Seventeen aircraft were lost in three years. How many do you suppose flew into what might be defined as a thunderstorm during that period? Seventy? Seven hundred? Seven thousand? Certainly it is safe to say that a lot more trespassed than were caught. This doesn't recommend the activity, but it does show that the error of entry is survivable, given a storm below the severe level and reasonable flying technique.

HANG IN THERE

The airplanes are strong. All they ask is to be flown at a speed that will give the structure maximum protection. Maneuvering speed makes this offer to the pilot: If the indicated airspeed is at or below that value, there is no way for a storm to break the airplane. When the airplane is at maneuvering speed, a vertical gust will cause the airplane to relieve itself (by momentarily stalling) as the limit-load factor is reached. At any speed above maneuvering, the airplane is vulnerable to an overstress situation. Below the speed, a vertical gust will make it stall at g-loads lower than the limit-load factor.

It is best to anticipate turbulence. If maneuvering speed is below normal cruise, slow the airplane to maneuvering at the first hint that turbulence might lie ahead. It is better to fly a few extra miles at reduced speed than to impose unnecessary stresses on the old airframe. Once the bumps start, the pilot's job description calls for wings to be kept level, the pitch attitude to be kept as close to level as possible, and the airspeed to be maintained somewhere around maneuvering speed. In light piston airplanes with rapid power response, the elevator is used to control pitch attitude, and power should be used freely when the airspeed shows a marked move away from maneuvering speed.

It must also be noted that maneuvering speed decreases as weight decreases. If only one maneuvering speed is listed in the pilot's operating handbook, and that speed is for gross weight, the airplane should be flown somewhat slower than the listed speed when penetrating turbulence at a lighter weight. A rule of thumb is to reduce the maneuvering speed by half the percentage the airplane is below gross weight. For example, if flying a 2,300-pound aircraft at 2,070 pounds, 10 percent below gross, reduce the published maneuvering speed by 5 percent.

CONTROVERSY

The mention of maneuvering speed being lower at lighter weights always causes some controversy. This is fact, though, for a number of reasons. One is that lower weights often result from fuel burn, which means that the spanwise distribution of weight has changed, with more weight concentration toward the center of the airframe and higher bending loads on the wings in turbulence. Also, the lighter airplane will experience more rapid acceleration when entering a vertical gust of given strength. And while the reduced weight might mean reduced bending loads on the wings in cases where the spanwise distribution of weight has not changed much, the sharper accelerations cause more stress on other parts of the airframe. Pilots tend to think only of the wings in turbulent situations; in truth, the wings are often the last parts to fail when an airplane breaks up in flight. For instance, the horizontal tail or an engine mount might fail first.

A garden-variety thunderstorm is a rough, wild, uncomfortable, and high-risk place to be in a light (or heavy) airplane, but it is not a hopeless place. If the pilot understands the factors working for and against success and keeps his or her act together, the airplane is likely to respond in kind.

VFR v. IFR

One rather interesting statistic might go here as well as anywhere else. As mentioned in Chapter 1, there are airframe failures in thunderstorms involving VFR pilots as well as IFR pilots. So, when you read of a thunderstorm accident, don't automatically consign it to an IFR pilot who flew into one and couldn't handle the situation.

You *can* almost consign each IFR thunderstorm accident to a pilot's failure to make every effort to stay out of storms. They just don't reach out, grab airplanes, and dash them to the ground. In a few cases, the pilot was receiving radar vectors from air traffic control radar, and on the surface this is perhaps a suggestion that the pilot was "trapped" even though he was using all available tools to avoid thunderstorm activity. Often, though, study shows that the pilot was trying to use radar advisories to penetrate areas of severe weather. This won't work every time with airborne weather radar, much less with traffic control radar. The rule is to stay twenty miles away from strong cells when severe weather is forecast, and five miles away from all thunderstorm activity. A controller vectoring an aircraft through a "light" spot may or may not be providing such separation from cells.

WEATHER AVOIDANCE EQUIPMENT

In the period used to compile Figure 2, airborne weather radar and a device called the Stormscope were just finding their way into single-engine airplanes. (Weather radar displays precipitation; the Stormscope displays the relative location of electrical discharges. Either can be correlated with the likely location of turbulence. Both require interpretive skills.) While some of the twins in the thunder column might well have had weather avoidance equipment, none of the singles were likely equipped. This could be part of the reason more singles than twins had thunderstorm problems and, as radar and Stormscope installations become more common in singles, this might change. But it might not. If pilots place too much faith in weather avoidance equipment and try to use it for weather penetration, throwing caution to the winds, thunderstorm problems could actually increase. It is true that airborne equipment can at times enable a pilot to weave through an area of activity, or find a gap in a line. And it is true that it helps in recognizing the possible and the impossible. But it in no way makes the impossible possible.

THE BIGGEST PROBLEM

Thunderstorms, like ice, command respect. Their menace is apparent, and warnings about staying away from them are plentiful. They rank high on the least-wanted list: Ask IFR pilots what bugs them most and it'll be thunder or ice, depending on the region of the country. In truth, though, these two things are only the tip of the iceberg. There are two silent and invisible IFR problems that account for almost 50 percent of the total IFR accidents—over twice as many as ice and thunderstorms combined. One reason they retain mastery over pilots is because they are not obvious. The severity can't be seen growing on the wing or flashing in the sky, and they can't be felt tossing the airplane about. For a fact, the instrument approach is the site of most IFR accidents, yet there are few pilots who are nearly as concerned about a low approach as they might be about a cumulonimbus ahead or a growing white line of ice on the leading edge. The next leading problem is a simple loss of control of the airplane.

NUMERO UNO

Virtually all instrument-approach accidents have something in common. For one reason or another, a pilot leaves the haven of a minimum safe altitude shown on a chart and then flies the brightly painted collection of aluminum into the earth. The reason is seldom related to the elements or to the machine. Instead, the approach accidents can almost all be charged either to poor procedures or to overzealousness.

Poor procedures? Certainly anything a pilot does that results in an accident is a poor procedure. But in IFR we find a special breed of procedural mistakes that is related to misreading or misunderstanding a chart. Some examples include an incorrect direction of turn on a missed approach, an attempted circling approach below circling minimums, or a descent to an altitude lower than the safe minimum on the chart. In the latter case, the reference is not to the final approach segment. When pilots descend below the minimum on final, I think it is almost always chargeable to overambition in wanting to find the ground and land, or to a reliance on visual flying when the actual clues are inadequate or misleading.

The chart-reading mistakes are in a minority on IFR

approach accidents, even though one of the more publicized airline accidents, the 1974 Thanksgiving weekend TWA crash near Dulles, was related to this problem. Still, reading a figure incorrectly can lead to serious consequences and is something to guard against.

ACCIDENTALLY ON PURPOSE

The nature of most IFR approach accidents strongly suggests that the descent was intentional. In some instances the pilot might break the rules by leaving the minimum descent altitude (or decision height if on an ILS) before sighting the runway, the approach lights, or other markings identifiable with the approach end of the runway. This takes a lack of imagination, because minimums provide truly minimum clearances over the ground and over obstacles. In most cases, the minimum altitudes flown during an IFR approach are actually much lower than a pilot would find comfortable, or would normally fly, in VFR weather. If a pilot tempted with "busting" minimums would take a moment to visualize the rocks and trees reaching hungrily for the belly of the airplane, such temptation might fade.

LOSS OF CONTROL

In research covering earlier periods, I failed to find a substantial number of accidents in which an instrument-rated pilot on an IFR flight plan apparently lost control of the airplane without the aid of a thunderstorm. But in this three-year period, it was a relatively frequent thing, with more twin than single involvement.

When considering a loss of control, it's natural first to think that something might have gone wrong with the instruments. Vacuum failure could have been a factor. But most twins have redundant systems, so this explanation wouldn't help much here. And in the mechanical (other than engine) column, where vacuum, electrical or instrument problems are included, we see the logical situation of more singles than twins.

What were the circumstances of the loss of control accidents? Some happened en route, but a much greater number happened on departure, approach, and missed approach. Perhaps this at least partly explains the predominance of twins. There's more to do, to distract, in a twin. And when you consider that the regulations permit a pilot to get an instrument rating in a simple single and then fly IFR in a twin (as long as he has a multiengine rating), there is even more logic to a predominance of loss-of-control accidents in twins.

In the mechanical column, singles predominate. Most were problems with the electrical or vacuum systems. In either case, it is possible to work around a failure of the system. Neither leaves the pilot instantly helpless in the typical failure. But the workload would surely increase and the pilot would have to make correct decisions quickly. With a vacuum failure, it is a matter of transitioning to partial panel flight and getting the airplane on the ground while flying without the artificial horizon and directional gyro, and probably without the autopilot. With an electrical

failure, which usually comes when the generator or alter-
nator fails and leaves the pilot with the energy in a fully
charged battery to parlay into view of a runway, recognition is the key. Catch it the moment of failure, and there
should be enough juice there to get a clearance for an approach to the nearest airport, and for navigation through
the approach. Certainly IFR is the worst time for either of
these systems to fail, but failure of the system shouldn't be
allowed to mandate an accident. Pilot proficiency at
handling the problem is the key.

ENGINE FAILURE

The relative merits of singles v. twins will be covered fully
in Chapter 8, but *what do you do if the engine quits*" is
such a common lament about single-engine IFR that it
should be addressed here as well. Nine twins were in fatal
accidents because an engine quit; one single was so involved in this period. If you add the four twins in fuel
exhaustion accidents (where *both* engines quit), the score
is thirteen to one. There is no available figure on IFR
hours, single and twin, to use in creating a true comparative number. However, consider that the fleet of singles
flying IFR is larger than the twin fleet. So even though each
twin averages more IFR hours annually, it becomes reasonable to assume that the IFR hours flown, single v. twin,
might be roughly equal. Twins probably do fly more IFR at
night, which factor would work against them because the
general accident rate is much worse at night.

The one-engine failure single in three years was a worst case situation: IFR, night, mountainous terrain, and the engine failed for mechanical reasons. There was no way to look at it and rationalize: "Oh, if the pilot had just done a good job on the forced landing, they would have been okay." It was probably a near-impossible situation. But isn't it remarkable that this happened only once in three years? That one lone accident compared with all the other IFR accidents, and compared with all the twins lost because of engine failure, strongly suggests that if pilots want to worry over risk in general aviation IFR flying, they had best worry about something other than engine failure in single-engine airplanes.

DEPARTURES

When a pilot flies into something on an IFR departure, with the aircraft in control, it's usually a simple matter of not following procedures and flying into high terrain, or of flying gradually into the ground or trees after departure. I suppose it could be argued that the latter is a loss of control —flight back into the trees would hardly be something you'd do on purpose—but when the airplane descends, wings level, into something, it is pretty much in control. This would be an area for the infrequent instrument pilot to watch carefully. That first entry into low clouds after a long period of IFR inactivity could be difficult.

Airframe failures in IFR conditions, with no thunderstorms around, are a relatively small part of the problem.

Because this subject is so often related to particular airplanes, it will be fully covered in Chapter 10.

In total, there's no mystery in the IFR accident picture. If there is any surprise, it's in the things pilots fear most—ice, thunder, and engine failures in singles—accounting for such a relatively small percentage of the total problem. Also, as we will see in the next chapter, the condition of light has a marked effect on the IFR accident record. This too should give us knowledge to use in minimizing risks while flying IFR.

3 | Night Flying

Night flying is one of the more utilitarian uses of the general aviation airplane, but many feel there is extra risk connected with flying around in the dark.

On the plus side, you can finish a day's work, fly into the night, and be at home or wherever else you might want to be the next morning. In many instances, a few hours of night flying can effectively save almost a whole day. Night flying can also cut travel costs by eliminating extra evenings with the innkeeper.

But isn't night flying foolhardy, especially in single-engine airplanes? If the engine quits, zap, you are zapped. Many a pilot has contemplated that unhappy event while gazing down into inky space and has forever sworn off the use of single-engine airplanes at night for fear of engine failure. That is an understandable human emotion, but it is without basis in fact. The things that hurt in the dark are seldom related to actual mechanical failure, and I've always wondered if perhaps the bad, the really bad accident rate at night might not have some relationship to pilot fear of engine failure in singles. There might be a widespread feeling that the engine is the only key to longevity when flying in the dark. There is nothing else to worry about as long as the engine runs. The record shows that such a feeling couldn't be further from the truth.

THE BIG PICTURE

The majority of serious night accidents are related to weather, not mechanical considerations. Almost 60 percent of the fatal night accidents involve weather. And in Figure 3, the stack of accidents representing attempted VFR flight in adverse weather conditions at night is an incredibly large part of the total weather-related VFR accident picture, especially when you consider that only about 10 percent of the VFR flight plans cover night flights. In this year, the same used for Figure 1 on page 21, almost half the "VFR in adverse weather" accidents were at night. In my studies of the subject, it appears that the night/weather problem is worsening steadily. And any way you look at the statistics and classify the accidents, night VFR cross-country flying in marginal weather comes up as *the highest risk form of general aviation flying*. Except in clear or near-clear conditions, night VFR flying is a very dangerous thing to do.

DOUBLE OBSCUREMENT

A lot of factors influence the risk involved in night VFR. The most important one is the simple fact that you can't see in the dark. This reduces night flying to instrument flying except on a clear night with a substantial moon and when flying over large, lighted metropolitan areas in good weather. Even if a pilot thinks he is flying VFR and is licensed only for VFR, survival depends on information from the instrument panel when it is really dark out. Avoiding terrain is a function of knowing terrain elevations and flying at a safe altitude, as indicated on the altimeter. Where a pilot might successfully hedgehop in the daytime by eyeball, seldom referring to the altimeter, the situation reverses at night. Then the altimeter and knowledge of position are prime considerations. The altimeter works as well at night, but consider the relative difficulty of keeping up with position at night. Pilotage navigation is highly approximate, and radio navigation is often of limited usefulness if flying low. Also, radio navigation would carry with it the requirement to correlate the position suggested by the equipment with the terrain.

NEXT KEY

Missing the terrain is only part of the night VFR problem, too. Another key to success is in staying out of cloud. Clouds, unfortunately, are not marked, and a VFR pilot

| VFR flying in adverse weather | | Alcohol or drug related | | Engine failure | | Landing | | Unwarranted low flying | |
TWIN	SNGL	TWIN	SNGL	TWIN	SNGL	TWIN	SNGL	TWIN	SNGL
	AA5B								
	AA5B								
	AA5A								
	AA5A								
	AA5A								
	AA1A								
	BE33								
	BE35								
	BE35								
	BE35								
	BE35								
	BE35								
	BE35								
	BL14								
	BL14								
	BL14								
	BL14								
	C150								
	C150								
	C152								
	C172								
	C172								
	C172								
	C172								
	C172								
	C177								
	C177								
	C177								
	C177								
	C182								
	C182								
	C182								
	C182								
	C182								
	C182								
	C182								
	C182								
	C185								
	C210								
	C210								
	MO20								
	MO20								
	NAVN								
	PA28		AA1A						
	PA28		C150						
	PA28		C150						
	PA28		C150						
	PA28		C150						
	PA28		C150						
BE18	PA28		C150						
BE95	PA28		C172						
B200	PA28		C172						
C310	PA28		C180						C150
C310	PA28		C182	BE58					C150
PA23	PA28		PAJ3	C310			BE35		C172
PA23	PA28		PA20	MTU2	C206	BE95	BL14		C182
PA30	PA32		PA28	PA31	M020	LJ23	C150		C206
PA30	PA32		PA28	PA31	PA22	PA23	C150		PA28
PA34	STNS	C310	TCFT	PA34	PA28	PA31	MO20	None	PA28

Figure 3. Night fatal accidents. One year.

Improper IFR operation		Pilot fatigue		Fuel exhaustion		Takeoff		Mechanical problems	
	BE23								
	BE33								
	BE35								
BE55	C172				AA1A				
BE58	C177				BE24				
BE90	C206				C206			BE18	
B200	MO20				PA22			C402	
PA23	PA28	BGLE	BE23		PA28		C172	C441	PA24
S226	R112	PA23	PA24	PA23	PA28	C414	C207	PA23	PA28
TWIN	SNGL	TWIN	SNGL	TWIN	SNGL	TWIN	SNGL	TWIN	SNGL

can inadvertently fly into cloud at night quite easily. The stage is then set for spatial disorientation and loss of control. Rain areas are also difficult to see in the dark.

PILOT EXPERIENCE

The experience level of pilots who unsuccessfully tangle with inclement weather at night adds an interesting piece to the puzzle. Half are pilots with less than 300 total flying hours, and quite a few are student pilots. That is a low experience level to pit against a cloudy night, and it seems almost possible to write this group off with one thought: They simply did not understand the difficulty of the task and the high risk involved.

In most cases nothing helped them understand because no night flying experience was required of private pilots for years. Then the rules were changed to require either three hours of night flying for private pilot applicants or a day-time-only license. A special requirement for at least ten night landings suggests that the Feds think landing the airplane is the toughest part of doing it in the dark. That's part of it, true, but landing at night is certainly less difficult than flying night VFR cross-country in marginal conditions.

The night and day legal VFR minimums are the same, too. This is an additional suggestion to a new pilot that there is no substantial difference between daylight and dark. Combine the lack of emphasis in training with the lack of regulatory guidance, and then the unfortunate night record and the involvement of relatively inexperienced pilots becomes more understandable. The minimum amount of instrument training required of new private pilots could also bear on this by making a pilot look on loss of visual reference as a somewhat less than critical matter.

PURPOSE

Almost three-fourths of the ill-fated night flights are for pleasure or personal transportation. This use accounts for 35 percent of the total general aviation cross-country flying. Three-fourths of the accidents on one-third of the flights suggest that there must be a strong connection between the two things. One might ask what the purpose of the night flight should have been to make it safer. Why do we fly better at night when on business than when flying for personal reasons? Perhaps it is because the pleasure user is trying to add something to his activity by flying at night, and the pressure to complete it without interfering with a primary activity is great. The business user flying at night is doing something that is related to a primary activity. Also, pleasure use might involve playfulness on local flights, and an airplane isn't a very safe nighttime toy.

It is noteworthy that in one year there were no night weather-related accidents in instructional flying. That perfect record might be an indication of an almost total lack of activity, a lack that sends new private pilots flying away on dark nights with little or no training.

SINGLE-ENGINE

The single-engine is predominant in night accidents. In most past studies I've done, the single's involvement was proportionately high as well. About 85 percent of the total airplanes are singles. In some years, substantially more than 85 percent of the airplanes involved in accidents at night were singles, but that picture seems to have changed. In the year covered by Figure 3, only 75 percent of the airplanes were singles. However, the typical night accident is not related to engines and the number of engines doesn't seem to matter. In Figure 3, twins outnumber singles 6:4 when it comes to fatal crashes after an engine failure at night.

The singles involved in weather-related night VFR accidents tend to be traveling-type airplanes: four-place with a generous number of retractables included. The load factor tends to be high, too, with an average of 2.35 people aboard the singles. The average load for single-engine airplanes in all cross-country operations is said to be 2.1.

HOLIDAYS AND WEEKENDS

Many weather-related night accidents are associated with weekends or holiday periods. That is a natural connection. Leave after work on Friday and return after playing all day on Sunday. Or do the same thing around a holiday. Put it all together—night, some passengers, the need to get back to work, and then throw in some weather along the way. The pressure on the pilot increases with each ingredient.

If you have a business appointment with John Smith at Monday noon and the morning dawns cloudy and cruddy, it isn't so difficult or awkward to call Smith and tell him the sad tale. But if you find yourself 300 cloudy and rainy miles from home and work at seven o'clock on Sunday evening and John Smith is your boss, the conversation with him might be more strained. All these factors clearly define a primary area for risk management.

NIGHT IFR

Whereas the weather-related night situation involving VFR flights is logical and relatively easy to rationalize, the IFR situation poses more questions. In the accident totals without regard to condition of light, we see IFR as a relatively low-risk, methodical operation. But when night is separated from day, the general aviation IFR pilot shows a clear weakness. The concept of matching numbers on the panel with numbers in the chart for good results doesn't do as well in the dark. From 10 to 15 percent of the IFR flights are flown at night, and almost 30 percent of the general aviation IFR accidents occurred at night during the one-year period covered by Figure 3.

The night IFR pilots who have problems bear no resemblance to their relatively inexperienced VFR counterparts.

In one year, pilots with over 10,000 total flying hours accounted for almost 20 percent of the night IFR accidents and outnumbered under-1,000-hour pilots by about 2:1 on the accident roster. Virtually all pilots involved in night IFR accidents held either commercial or airline transport pilot certificates, with the latter august group accounting for 30 percent of the problems. Most of the airplanes were twins.

EXPLANATION?

There doesn't seem to be any quick explanation for the night IFR accidents. The mail pilots flying old twin Beeches don't show up in great numbers, nor do the people flying checks and packages to and fro across the country at all hours of the night. These people fly night IFR a lot, and they know how to do it. The division of IFR airplanes between singles and twins appears logical enough. Heavier twins probably fly more at night than any others, getting executives home after a full day's work at a faraway place, so you'd expect to find some of them here. Retractable singles are more likely flown IFR and at night, to realize return from a relatively large investment, so they show up as a high percentage of the airplanes in that column of Figure 3.

We noted that a high percentage of the pilots involved in accidents while flying VFR into adverse weather at night were on pleasure or personal transportation missions. There is no such corner on the night IFR accident market, where the uses are almost equally divided among personal transportation, business, corporate (meaning flights with a hired pilot), and air taxi cargo and passenger flights. This cross-section eliminates any thought about a strong correlation between night IFR and type of use. Despite its regimentation and procedure, IFR is just one of those things that the general aviation pilot doesn't do as well in the dark.

The instrument approach is, as you might expect, the site of most night IFR accidents. The "premature arrival," as it is often called, reaches a peak after sunset. A contributing factor (but no excuse) is the lack of precision approach facilities with glide path guidance at general aviation airports. Also, many of the approaches call for circling. It has always seemed to me that a night circling approach in precipitation is the most exacting procedure in flying, and the record tends to support this theory. Perhaps the night IFR pilot really has the same trouble as the night VFR pilot because the last portion of the approach, after breaking out of the clouds, is really a rather difficult version of marginal VFR.

ILLUSIONS

Visual cues at night are purely lousy, and if one key factor could be assigned to night IFR approach difficulties it would probably have to be pilot reliance on erroneous visual cues. At the trying time after transitioning from instruments to visual flying, the only lights that can really help a pilot judge the descent are the lights on the runway of intended landing. Even the full approach lighting system on an ILS cannot help a pilot judge a descent angle. Why? It is a matter of the aiming point supplying the only valid visual cue on a visual approach. And if the aiming point is not the end of the runway, then the pilot is about to make the National Transportation Safety Board's computer whirl for a millisecond to count off one more who disregarded that fact. A pilot who leaves the safety of a minimum descent height or decision height at night without the runway lights in sight is looking for trouble.

According to the good book, the approach lights or any other marking identifiable with the end of the runway are excuse enough to descend. But if you want to preserve the old tail, insist on the runway itself, because all that's legal isn't safe.

ILLUSIONS PLUS TEMPTATIONS

The nature of lights can lead a pilot down a perilous path at night, too. For example, you might shoot an approach, still be in cloud, and yet catch glimpses of the lights as the runway is overflown. This suggests that another try might be in order, perhaps at a somewhat lower altitude. That is a risky temptation and one that might not appear in the daytime when nothing but a gray mass would be sliding beneath the airplane as it plunges merrily through the murk. Some say that night approaches are easier because lights tend to be more visible than, say, just a runway by day.

They might be easier to see, but what you see can hurt instead of help unless the limitations of the visual cue are recognized.

I think it a good reminder for day or night IFR to occasionally shoot approaches in good weather with no hood on. The descent to the minimum altitude, and flight at that altitude in visual conditions, is always a good illustration of how close you are to the ground when level at the minimum descent altitude or decision height. Then when shooting an approach to Jackass Flat on some dark and rainy night you can think back to what it looked like in daytime visual conditions. That should be enough to discourage any thoughts of a premature descent.

THUNDER AND LIGHTNING

The annual night IFR accident sample is small enough that some variations do occur. In one year I found almost no thunderstorm-related night accidents; in another year thunderstorms were factors in a substantial percentage of the night IFR accidents. The strongest thought here is that storms are equally mean day or night and that while you might think they would be easier to avoid at night (because lightning is visible), there is probably no appreciable difference in the avoidance chore that might be based on the condition of light. True, at night you can always fly with the lightning at your back and avoid storms. But it is equally true that you can always fly with the cauliflower-shaped or dark clouds at your back in the daytime and

avoid thunderstorms. I doubt if many pilots have flown into
a cumulonimbus day or night without at least some knowledge that one was around and some apprehension about the
hue of the sky, be it illuminated by lightning at night, or
dark and ominous by day.

WEATHER SUMMARY

IFR or VFR, the record is clear in showing that the general
aviation pilot manages risks poorly when combining
weather and night flying.

There is no solution as such to the night VFR weather
question, avoidance is the only key. The wise VFR pilot
would limit night cross-country flights to much better than
minimum VFR weather, preferably clear skies, and would
rely on the altimeter and not the eyeball for terrain clearance. A guideline might be never to fly lower than 2,000
feet above the highest obstacle within ten miles of the proposed flight path. If that can't be done at night in good
VFR conditions, then it's time to be on the ground.

The IFR pilot's primary goal should be awareness of
visual limitations at night. Not leaving the minimum
descent altitude or the decision height until the runway
lights are in sight is a good guard against the most common
night IFR problems.

The night IFR pilot should also realize that the activity is
one that few pilots engage in very often. Thus there are not
many people who are really proficient at night IFR. Total
flying experience just doesn't count for much when you are

groping around the airport in the dark trying to line up with a runway. This is the most difficult maneuver; it is probably also the least practiced one. Few pilots get hood practice at night, and I don't know that it would be a very good simulation anyway. The message is to recognize the risks in night IFR and avoid them in a methodical manner.

THE OTHER ITEMS

In discussing IFR and VFR weather-related problems, we've covered a majority of the night fatal accidents. A substantial percentage of the remaining night fatals involve one of the easiest risks of all to manage, alcohol. There aren't as many drunk-pilot accidents as some sources would suggest, but there are still enough to recognize this as a problem. The drinking-pilot phenomenon will be discussed fully in Chapter 12. More of these accidents happen at night simply because that is when many people do their drinking. Once the alcohol has been consumed and the airplane mounted, the condition of light doesn't have much to do with the outcome.

FUEL EXHAUSTION

Fuel exhaustion is another clearly identifiable cause of serious accidents at night. This is perplexing. If pilots are apprehensive about engine failures when flying at night, logic would suggest very conservative fuel reserves. The record, though, shows that there might be relatively more serious fuel exhaustion accidents at night than in the daytime. A lot of this is no doubt due to the fact that a forced landing at night is more serious than in the daytime, but you'd still think that it is something that would almost never happen. The fact that it does is yet another sad commentary on the thought processes of some general aviation pilots.

Fuel exhaustion is a clear example of how the disciplines of flying work. Every year about 200 general aviation pilots have an accident (not all are serious) after running out of fuel. Airline pilots seldom do it, though in recent years there was one fuel exhaustion fatal accident (a DC-8 at Portland, Oregon), and one well-publicized case of a 747 running out on the runway after landing. There were extenuating circumstances in both cases—a landing gear problem with the DC-8 and below forecast weather and traffic problems with the 747—but pilots are trained and paid to keep extenuating circumstances from ending in accidents.

Still, airline pilots do well at landing with fuel in the tanks and general aviation pilots do not. Why? Simple—airline pilots don't kid themselves about fuel, and they have the checks and balances of a dispatch system. There is a required reserve and this reserve is not to be violated. An air carrier might hold for improvement in weather, but when the moment comes that the holding is about to dip into the required reserve, it's off to the alternate, no question. In contrast, the general aviation pilot's only checks and balances are in thoughts of what it might be like to run out of fuel. Some pilots apparently lack imagination. And while most fuel exhaustion accidents involve singles, some involve twins. That would have to be one of life's dumbest feelings: Fly a twin because of a feeling that the engine-out capability might be useful and then use all the gas.

WHY?

The reasons pilots run out of fuel at night are not valid, but they are factors and must be considered. To begin with, it is more difficult to buy fuel at night. Most airports close at sundown, so the night flier must plan refueling stops carefully or wind up with a long way to go on a little fuel. Some fuel exhaustion accidents happen after relatively short flights that started with limited fuel on board, but most come after long flights.

Intentions are probably tolerable at the start of most fuel exhaustion flights. For example, the airplane holds four plus thirty worth of fuel; the time to the destination will be four hours, so that's thirty minutes extra. If there is a headwind, a stop can be made at Podunk just before dark to fly on with full tanks.

The real facts can become obscured as such a flight progresses, though. Perhaps the ground speed is three knots less than that used in calculating the thirty-minute reserve. Make the fuel stop based on that fact, or keep on flying and see? Maybe it gets dark a little earlier than anticipated and Podunk doesn't answer the Unicom when called. Landing and finding no fuel might mean either delaying until the next morning or finding someone to come out and fill the tanks. Press on. The accident investigators often note that a pilot bypassed several lighted airports at night before using all the fuel and settling ignominiously into the darkness below. You do, however, have to recognize the fact that most of those airports were unattended at the time, and a landing would leave the airplane on a dark ramp with only the attention of the airport cat. The pilot knew that and it would have to be recognized as a factor. It is not a valid excuse for running out of fuel at night; it is just one of the reasons pilots do it.

LOST?

The relative difficulty of night navigation is another reason pilots run out of fuel at night. If a pilot flies with a thirty-minute reserve and he can't find the destination airport immediately, a very difficult situation arises.

One moral is that thirty minutes' fuel reserve is never enough. That is true day or night. We should really fly with a full and fat one-hour reserve calculated for every flight. That reserve should be considered an inviolate supply for emergency use only. No fair using even one pint of it to go on in the face of a slightly stronger-than-forecast headwind. Reserve fuel is for use when all else fails, for when the weather does an unforecast dirty trick, for when navigational ability fails you, or for when some mechanical problem introduces time-consuming procedure to the flight. The only proper pilot action when considering the use of reserve fuel for the normal part of a flight is to say: "This is stupid. We're going to make a fuel stop."

Fuel exhaustion is simply a product of the pilot's failure to think. Once I dug out a figure that is interesting to contemplate. In a large group of night accidents, the consequences of a forced landing at night after fuel exhaustion tended to be more serious than the consequences of forced landing after mechanical failure (which doesn't happen very often). Could it be that the pilot felt rather dumb after making the mistake of using all the fuel and could not perform in the forced landing?

MISMANAGEMENT

Another problem can come with fuel on board, but with the engine sucking on a dry tank or even on no tank. There are instances of a pilot actually turning the fuel off when intending to switch to the fullest tank or tanks before landing. This type of mistake tends to be serious when the pilot does it at an altitude too low to permit recognition and correction of the mistake. That bears a rather plain message: Take care of the tank switching at altitude, especially at night.

THE NITTY-GRITTY

Rare indeed are night forced landings that are a product of true mechanical failure as opposed to fuel mismanagement, exhaustion or contamination; carburetor impact icing, or other such pilot-related things. In fact, they account for a relatively insignificant percentage of the serious and total night accidents. For a look at the total picture (as opposed to fatal accidents only) I examined 130 night accidents and found the following engine failure involvement: an engine failure on takeoff followed by a safe landing; an internal failure of the engine followed by a safe landing; an engine fire followed by a successful on-airport landing; an engine failure for unknown reasons after which the pilot ditched in a river and swam to shore; a safe freeway landing after a failure for unknown reasons; a slide off the end of the runway after a failure on takeoff; and a double engine failure caused by jet fuel in piston engines followed by a successful landing. "Safe" or "successful" means there was no personal injury. In each of these accidents, the engine apparently failed for reasons reasonably beyond the pilot's control, at least his control in the cockpit. To give some comparison of what happens when the pilot fouls up, there were twenty-five fuel mismanagement or exhaustion night accidents in the same sample: four of the twenty-five were fatal.

PROPELLERS

A rather unusual accident crops up often enough at night to warrant special note. Instances of passengers walking into propellers shows up three times in the 130-accident sample just noted. Needless to say, the results are always serious. It is difficult to imagine why this might happen more at night unless there is a tendency to let passengers get out while the engine is still running to go turn on car or hangar lights. Whatever, it is bad practice to let a passenger enter or leave an airplane with the engine running. An exception might be a twin, with the engine on the door side secured but the other one running. Even then, it would be unwise to let someone not familiar with flying machinery do much moving around the airplane when an engine is running.

APPROACH AND LANDING

Approach and landing accidents in good weather are quite common at night and can be serious. Most of the total accidents happen during the landing itself; the serious ones usually come when the pilot misjudges the approach and hits something short of the runway.

TAKE CAREFUL AIM

The principles of flying to a runway are the same, day or night, fair weather or foul. It is a fact that the point on the ground toward which the airplane is flying remains stationary in the windshield as the airplane is flown at a constant attitude. Change attitude and the constant spot changes its position in the windshield. Change power or

descend into a level with a different wind component, and
things will change, but again one spot will appear to remain
constant to the eye and the airplane will be tracking toward
that spot. The runway lights make this rather easy to see at
night.

THE SLOPE

The protected slope for obstruction clearance on VFR approaches is supposed to be 20:1. That ratio applied to a
ninety-knot ground speed means that a 456-foot-per-
minute rate of descent will maintain standard obstacle
clearance. Since all airports don't meet the protected slope,
it would be good to add 50 percent to the minimum rate of
descent and use a 700-fpm rate of descent on a ninety-knot
approach to a VFR runway. The interaction between this
and the constant spot theory is what keeps you out of the
trees on dark nights. For example, if the spot remains constant with the airspeed on ninety knots, but the rate of
descent is less than the acceptable amount (700 feet per
minute), then the approach path is too shallow. Add some
power and fly up to a steeper slope before resuming the
descent.

(It's simple to determine the required rate of descent for
a 20:1 slope. Convert speed to feet per minute and then
divide by 20.)

IFR runways have a required 34:1 protected slope, so
the situation is not as critical there, but it is good practice
always to use a uniform approach slope at night for visual

approaches. And the slope should be as steep as is safely practical in the type of aircraft flown.

WHAT IF?

One question always emerges toward the end of a discussion about the risks involved in night flying. Even though it is true that virtually all the engine failures at night are pilot induced, involving mismanagement of fuel or running out of gas, there is still some remote possibility that an essential engine part will give up the ghost and the cabin of a single-engine airplane will become quiet even though the pilot has done everything right. What then? It is easy to sit on the ground and pontificate over engines not quitting, but what do you do when one *does* fail at night?

THERE IS HOPE

I suppose it is best to realize first that things are not hopeless. A very high percentage of the night forced landings are both survivable and survived. One key would be in touching down at minimum speed, but not stalling the airplane prematurely and reaching the ground in a spin or with a high sink rate. Another would be in not hitting some fixed object at a right or even a steep angle. Any stop will be very uncomfortable if it is sudden, but if the deceleration is spread over a period of time things won't be so bad.

I've heard it suggested that dark areas without lights might be cleared fields, good for night landings. They might be in Kansas, but in Arkansas such an area might more likely be forested or mountainous. At least it would be free of houses or power lines, though.

What if it is a mountain? Then it would be important to know the general ridge orientation in the area. You would certainly fare better coming down on a heading parallel to the ridges rather than doing it at right angles. This all suggests that pilot knowledge of the terrain is part of risk management at night.

In studying the charts to gain knowledge of the terrain, it is often possible to plan a route that will have inherent advantages. One night run I make frequently can be done one of two ways: Fly direct over some dark and rough terrain, or fly the north airway, only five miles longer, and stay within gliding distance of a river valley and four-lane highway all the way. It doesn't take much imagination to select the proper path.

WHERE TO?

After a power failure the first impulse is to pick a place to go. Unless the goal is something that is easily identifiable, such as a four-lane highway, chances are that no really intelligent selection of landing area will be possible early in the glide from a normal cruising altitude at night. An exception would be with a moon or with an overcast and a lot of light reflection off the clouds over a populated area.

Then something might be chosen early. In any case, turning the cockpit lights down to a very dim setting would help improve night vision. There are some things to do, too. Inform someone of the plight on the radio if possible, and try to get the engine going again. Switch mags, experiment with the mixture and the fuel selector, check the primer as locked, run the fuel pump, and do anything else that might change the status quo. Also, look for an airport. You'd sure hate to make a night forced landing in a random area if a lighted airport was within gliding distance.

How far can you glide? The glide ratio is in the pilot's operating handbook. It is a good thing to commit to memory.

At lower altitudes, landing lights can be a good aid in a night forced landing. How do you use them? The old joke is to turn them on and, if you don't like what you see, then turn them off. The value of the lights, though, is in giving the pilot last-minute choices. With lights plus the energy stored in a normal glide you can turn a little, flare, and keep flying to the last moment while remembering that the outcome will be successful if that sudden stop can be avoided. I would add that in such a situation a shoulder-harness system would be worth its weight in diamonds.

FATIGUE

When assigning accident causes, the National Transportation Safety Board probably cites fatigue only when it is clear-cut. If, for example, it is known that the pilot had little sleep in the last twenty-four hours, it might well be considered a factor in the accident. So the small stacks in Figure 3's fatigue column might be considered as representing obvious, almost extreme, cases. Lower levels of fatigue are bound to be a factor in many more night accidents.

Even night people start running out of zip at some point in the evening, and there's probably an hour past which a person shouldn't fly. The old brain just gets too dull. I went one night with a friend of mine who spent his evening flying cancelled checks about in an Aerostar. The airplane was stripped inside, and was noisy enough to make you tired in an hour. Not being a day sleeper, I had been unable to rest much before starting out at 6 P.M. By midnight I was very tired. I felt like a zombie for the early morning segment of the flight. He was used to it, I wasn't. Every pilot should probably put some limit on the day's effort—the combination of work or play and flying—and be on the ground after that much activity. Disregard of such a limit followed by an accident might not be charged to fatigue, but the pilot's mental and physical state could make a strong contribution to a descent below decision height or a foolish decision to press on VFR into adverse weather.

THE END OF A PERFECT DAY

Flying through the sunset and into the night is an experience that only pilots appreciate fully. It is interesting that the impact of the beauty of a day's retreat over the horizon is evident on the radio. The chatter almost always fades away as the sun sets. It is a reflective moment, during which a person is thankful for life and for the freedom of flight. After the beauty of the moment, though, carry on with the thought that it is a good thing to do only if the risks are recognized and managed, so that you may enjoy the sunrise, which is an equally beautiful time to reflect on the beauty of life and flight.

4 | Wind

Wind is natural to an airplane. After all, the only purpose of the propeller is to pull the machine forward and make wind over the wings. Wind can be weather, though, especially to the light airplane. It can have profound effects on the airplane as it moves up, down, and around. Just to play with words, it could even be said that wind is the number one hazard associated with thunderstorms. Those vertical currents that jab are, after all, only wind that is headed up or down. The same currents flow out of the storm, rearrange themselves parallel with the ground, and become the first gust and strong sustained wind found at the surface in a thunderstorm area.

Those winds are considered part of the thunderstorm subject. Just plain wind is also a factor in airplane accidents, and while the most frequent wind-related accident is found during landing, the breeze does its thing at other times. Strong winds across mountains can create turbulence. Strong headwinds can menace the fuel supply. Strong crosswinds can have a deleterious effect on takeoff and climb performance. Wind shear—changes in wind direction and velocity with altitude—can play strange and potentially lethal tricks.

How many accidents are attributable to wind? It is listed by name as a cause or factor in about 7 percent of the accidents. Wind, or the pilot's failure to understand wind, is probably a factor in more accidents than that, though. Some stall/spin accidents might be related to wind, and approach and landing accidents, in which a pilot misjudges distance and lands short, might be attributable to wind shear more often than the records indicate. It should also be noted that general aviation flying tends to diminish when the wind blows. Just compare the activity at the local airport on a very windy Sunday with the activity on a calm and beautiful Sunday. The bending rate per hour flown is undoubtedly much higher when the wind is blowing.

HOW MUCH WIND?

At what point does wind start becoming a real factor in general aviation operations? The answer to that question depends on several things. One is very simple: It is what you are accustomed to in the way of wind. In sections of the country where the wind often blows with vigor, pilots tend to continue routine operations in conditions that might not be considered acceptable in areas where strong wind isn't such a day-to-day event. One school I know of in windy country routinely allows solo student operations in Cessna 150's when the wind is as high as twenty-five knots. Dual flying is allowed in winds up to thirty-two knots. Some pilots might find those values uncomfortable, but if the airplane is properly handled they are really quite safe.

I've always wondered at what precise point we find true additional risk in high wind operations. When the wind is strong enough to rock the airplane around on the ground, it suggests that at some point the machine and the wind will do their thing. And you do occasionally hear of an airplane being blown over. But in exploring such incidents, there often seems to be a contributing factor, such as fast taxiing. The exact point at which you quit flying because of wind is thus a highly individual judgment. It is based on the airplane, the pilot, the airport, and, I suppose, also on the need to fly. The turbulence associated with high winds is often uncomfortable enough to answer the question for you and prompt the delay of a trip that isn't of great importance.

WHAT DOES IT DO?

How does wind twist our tail when we bite off a bit too much of it? Starting at the beginning of a flight, there are some losses of directional control during crosswind take-offs. Many thought that the advent of the tricycle-gear airplane would solve the directional control accident problem, but it did not. There's no magic to a tricycle; if you let the machine go its own way in a strong crosswind, it'll try the ditch every time.

The serious wind-related accidents in the departure phase usually come after takeoff, during the initial climb. Where there is trouble it often comes with a strong crosswind on an airport of marginal length for the operation. Obstructions upwind from the runway often add spice by making the gusty wind flow even more turbulent.

The problem here is caused by several things. For one, even if the crosswind is precisely steady in direction and velocity, the airplane's takeoff roll will be longer than in a calm wind condition. There is aerodynamic drag associated with the corrections necessary to offset the crosswind, and it is also an item of good practice to accelerate to a slightly higher-than-normal speed before lift-off in a crosswind.

VARIABLE AND GUSTY

No strong crosswind provides an idyllic, steady, wind situation, and the variation in wind speed and direction might serve to prolong the takeoff even more. Any pilot who has flown much has experienced the crosswind situation in which the airspeed simply does not seem to increase for a moment during the takeoff run. In that situation, the wind direction has shifted more away from the nose of the airplane, or the velocity of a cross headwind has decreased. Things like this can happen at just the wrong time.

Once off the ground, the airplane is still subject to harassment by a strong crosswind. Wind just does not become steady and lose its gusty and shifty characteristics at a low altitude.

This is an appropriate place to address the subject of the wind's effect on an airplane in flight because wind can be used to advantage in the first stages of a climb, or it can be misunderstood to the point that the pilot's misuse of the airplane relative to the wind can result in an accident.

THE DOWNWIND TURN

The theory that the downwind turn is lethal has been the subject of much debate over the years. The argument is that once the airplane is free of the ground, a steady wind has no effect on airspeed whatsoever. Point it any way you wish, make 360s in strong winds; regardless of what you do the airspeed will not be affected by the wind. The ground track will be affected, to be sure, but the airspeed will remain constant. That is all very true. The other argument is that a low-altitude downwind turn will bite. That is also correct. For one thing, the low-level wind is seldom steady, and a gusty or variable wind does affect airspeed. For another, visual illusions lead a pilot to do the wrong things in a downwind turn.

This accident is a good illustration. It involved a go-around rather than a departure, but the principles are the same.

The crosswind was quite strong, and after aborting the landing attempt, the pilot elected to make a turn when a few hundred feet above the ground. The turn was in the normal traffic pattern direction, which just happened to be downwind. The airplane was not far into the turn when the angle of bank started increasing. Soon afterward, the airplane stalled and spun out of the bottom of the turn. The pilot was a victim of the downwind turn.

THE FACTORS

Examine the things that happen in such a situation. First, turning downwind close to the ground has an immediate and dramatic visual effect. As the airplane turns, the groundspeed increases rapidly. Even if the wind is perfectly steady, and the airspeed and vertical speed are in fact unaffected, the increase in groundspeed will result in a much flatter climb gradient relative to the ground and any obstructions. The eye doesn't lie in telling the pilot about more forward speed and a flatter climb gradient relative to the ground. The eye does, however, make a very bad suggestion in such a case: It suggests that the nose of the aircraft should be pulled up to maintain the climb gradient. That is definitely not the right thing to do when airspeed might be critical.

Strong wind is never completely steady, and the nature of wind relative to the ground couples with the illusion of a downwind turn to give a downwind turn just that much more lethal potential. Wind velocity tends to increase with altitude, so as the airplane climbs it is not operating in a steady wind. It might instead be flying with an increasing tailwind component, which causes some actual airspeed decay simply because the airplane does not adjust to the increase in wind instantly. Think of it like this: The airplane is flying at ninety knots indicated airspeed with a ten-knot crosswind. The groundspeed is about ninety knots. Turn downwind, climb, and suddenly increase that tailwind to thirty knots. What item is going to be most subject to immediate change? The airspeed. It won't drop an amount equal to the full increase in tailwind component, but it will drop some. The groundspeed of the airplane was at 100, as the turn was completed and the airplane must accelerate to reflect the tailwind component and the 130-knot groundspeed that would result as the climb continued. Acceleration does not happen instantly, and the difference between the time it takes the tailwind component to increase and the time it takes the airplane to accelerate is some indication of the sag a pilot might see and feel when maneuvering into an increasing tailwind component. If the airplane is climbing, there might not be any more power to use in this acceleration. The only solution would be to lower the nose, further flattening the climb gradient. It takes discipline to do that, but it is important because if the airspeed is low to begin with, as in a climb, any airspeed decay moves the airplane into a higher drag condition nearer to the stall.

QUESTION

Here we must digress for a moment to cover one question regarding the danger of a downwind turn. The increasing tailwind/decreasing airspeed business might lead you to believe that a steady wind does affect airspeed after all. When the airplane turns downwind in a steady wind, it is flying into an increasing tailwind, isn't it? Yes. But airspeed wouldn't be affected. The reason the airspeed is not affected turning downwind in a steady wind is because the airplane has already made its peace with the existing wind. The ground track was already affected by the crosswind (drift), and in a steady wind that effect simply translates to increased groundspeed as the airplane turns downwind—without bothering the airspeed. Wind affects airspeed only in gusty or gradient wind situations, when the actual direction or velocity of the wind changes abruptly.

Finally, as the airplane is banked for the downwind turn, one wing is actually at a higher altitude than the other and might be reaching up into a stronger wind. This would promote a strong overbanking tendency. Perhaps this seems farfetched in an airplane with a thirty-five-foot wingspan, where the actual altitude difference of the wing tips in a thirty-degree bank would be only 17.5 feet. But the theory is valid, and there have been times when I think I've seen this effect in a downwind turn.

UPWIND TURNS

Most of the factors that work against the pilot in a downwind turn work *for* the pilot in an upwind turn. Effective risk management in a strong crosswind situation thus suggests that any turns be made into the wind until at an altitude where the airspeed is at a very healthy value and climb capability is not critical.

EN ROUTE

What does wind do to you en route? The obvious things are related to groundspeed and comfort. The forecast winds aloft are often terribly inaccurate, and it is the pilot's responsibility to determine actual winds and not fly into a low-fuel situation because of a bad wind forecast.

Wind-induced turbulence can make the ride very uncomfortable—the stronger the wind, the worse the bumps, with the ante raised in direct proportion to the roughness of the terrain over which the wind is blowing.

As a strong wind blows over mountains, it can create turbulence so severe that it feels like the feathers are about to be plucked from the airplane's backside. Does such turbulence ever break an airplane? It can, to be sure, but it doesn't often do so. In one year there was but a single case of turbulence in clear air causing a serious general aviation accident.

Comfort is one reason we tend to stay out of real trouble in clear air turbulence. It becomes extemely uncomfortable in the airplane long before any structural limit is reached, and as a result, the pilot is likely to slow the airplane down. Slowing down reduces the g-forces encountered at a given bump, and this serves the purpose of giving the structure even more margin, as well as contributing to occupant comfort. Maneuvering speed should be used whenever turbulence becomes uncomfortable.

DOWNDRAFTS

When flying in mountainous terrain, wind-induced turbulence might be the most obvious problem to the seat of the pants, but downdrafts on the lee side of the mountains can be an even greater hazard. It is not uncommon to see downdrafts that can exceed the rate of climb in general aviation airplanes, even over such relatively small mountains as the Appalachians. Both turbulence and downdraft considerations suggest that mountainous terrain be avoided when the forecast wind at ridge level is thirty knots or greater, unless the flight can be made at an altitude of at least 50 percent higher than the ridge levels. That does not guarantee a smooth ride, but it does help minimize risk.

THE ARRIVAL

Wind does its thing on departure and en route, but the arrival is where wind is likely to bring the most sweat to the palms of a pilot. The last phase of the flight is probably the most turbulent of all when surface winds are high, and if the pilot doesn't make a conscious effort to relax, the flying begins to resemble a wrestling match between airplane and pilot more than anything else. This serves to increase tension, and by the time the airplane is in the pattern, the stage might be set for error.

Wind effects in the traffic pattern have a definite bearing on a safe arrival when using a runway with a strong crosswind component. For example, consider a runway that runs to the north, Runway 36, in a situation with a strong westerly wind—a rather common situation behind a cold front. If the pattern is left-hand, as most are, there will be a strong crosswind component from the right on downwind leg. The heading required will be 200 degrees if twenty degrees of drift is present. Then, on base leg, there will be a tailwind, if indeed a base leg is managed. Why trouble with base leg? For one thing, a turn of more than 180 degrees from the downwind leg heading will be required to bring an airplane around to a heading that will track the final approach course. If there's twenty degrees of drift on downwind, at least that much will be present on final, so the required turn from downwind to final will be 220 instead of 180 degrees.

OVERSHOT TURN

A tailwind on base will also tend to make the pilot overshoot the turn on final. As that starts to unfold, the strong tendency is to steepen the turn, hasten it on around. Perhaps a little bottom rudder might help. A bit more, and a little steeper bank. Whoops, it spun. Do it every time in such a situation.

Even though wind is not noted as a cause or factor in the accident report, it is often possible to find very serious accidents that were prompted, promoted, or caused by a strong downwind component on base leg. There are two ways to manage this risk. Either fly a very wide pattern, and fly with a firm resolve to go around if it appears that the turn onto final isn't working well. Or go against the grain and fly the pattern in the other direction, so that base leg will be into the wind. The latter might be contrary to the regulation requiring all turns to the left at uncontrolled airports unless otherwise stipulated, but in extreme conditions such action could be covered by the pilot's right to deviate from any rule as required to meet an emergency. Avoiding a situation where a stall/spin might occur would seem to be "meeting an emergency."

APPROACH SPEED

Once the traffic pattern has been carefully planned, the next thing is to select the final approach speed. The most common error here is to use too much speed. As the airplane squirms, writhes, pitches, and rolls in low-level turbulence on a windy day, we all tend to add too much extra speed to compensate. The result is an arrival a few feet above the runway with a lot of extra airspeed. At that point, the pilot faces a dilemma: The speed must be dissipated for a proper landing or, as an alternative, the airplane must be flown onto the runway at a higher-than-normal speed. A great number of landing accidents in high wind conditions are associated with the choice of the latter method of landing.

What is a proper approach speed in gusty conditions? The normal approach speed plus the difference between the steady wind and the peak gust is a maximum. Any speed higher than that would have to be considered excessive. Some just add half the difference between the steady wind and the peak gust, and that is generally adequate except in extreme conditions.

HOW IT'S DONE

How do pilots wreck airplanes after an approach at an excessive speed? One way is to run off the end of the runway, though if the wind is anything other than ninety degrees across the runway, the wind helps on cutting the required runway length after a fast approach. The more common way to bend the airplane comes after a crosswind landing in a tricycle-gear airplane with an improper distribution of weight on the wheels—meaning a concentration of weight on the nose rather than the main gear. In extreme cases, the nosewheel contacts the runway while the mains are still airborne. Nose gear assemblies tend to be less stout than the mains, and there's but one gear there whereas there are two at the rear. It is obvious that the main gear should take the brunt of anything and that doing it backward can only result in damage.

If the nose gear is subjected to enough abuse on landing, it will fail. Or it might maintain an outward appearance of health while the firewall, to which many nosewheels are attached, bends. Either event is expensive.

WHEELBARROWING

In instances where the nosewheel survives the initial onslaught, the improper weight distribution on the wheels of a tricycle can still master the pilot. The phenomenon is called *wheelbarrowing,* and anyone who has ever crashed with an overloaded wheelbarrow knows how it works. The weight is forward and steering is difficult, if not impossible. With weight in a tricycle-gear airplane forward, the pivot point is at the front, and there's just no way to have much influence on where the airplane goes in such a situation. Steering is based on having weight on the rear wheels, and steering is very important in a crosswind.

A couple of items of technique can help minimize the risks in a crosswind touchdown and rollout.

First, use the minimum possible flap setting. That often means no flaps in some light airplanes. You can touch on the rear wheels first at a higher speed when flaps are not used, and control effectiveness will thus be better both before and after touchdown. This isn't applicable on very short airports, but if the runway is short and the crosswind strong, it is time to go somewhere else anyway. If the pilot's operating handbook does not specify an approach speed when flaps are not used, try 1.3 times the flaps-up stalling speed and then add an appropriate amount for gusts.

The other technique item is something to remember *not*

to do. When landing in a crosswind (or at any time, for that matter), the thought should be that the elevator control is being brought aft. It should *not* be pushed forward once the airplane is close to the runway, in the landing process. If the airplane balloons up, just stop moving the wheel aft. Use a little power if the balloon is high, the airspeed is low, and the airplane feels as if it is about to develop a very high sink rate. But leave the elevator alone until the airplane is back close to the runway, then start working on the aft movement again. Charging the mind with such a thought will keep you away from a porpoising situation where the airplane might contact the runway and bounce, and bounce, and bounce, with the pilot moving the elevator control out of phase with the bounces and concentrating the force of contact on the nosewheel each time. Such maneuvers tend to get worse instead of better and go on to a conclusion. (The only exception to this is in a wheel landing in a conventional gear airplane, where the wheel must be moved forward at the moment of touchdown.)

GO AROUND?

Fortunately, landing accidents are not often serious. The situation can, however, become serious if the pilot does not exercise a measure of discipline and resist any temptation to go around late in an attempted landing.

There are two prime reasons a pilot might elect to go around. If the crosswind seems like it is more than might be manageable as the airplane is flared a few feet above the runway, it can prompt thoughts about going around. So can excessive use of runway for the slowing process before landing. There is, however, a point beyond which a go-around shouldn't be attempted. It is good to stake out that point early in the approach. On one airport that I use (single north/south runway, 3,000 feet long with a taxiway a few hundred feet south of the midpoint), I approach in strong crosswinds with the firm resolve to go around if the rear wheels are not firmly on the ground when passing the taxiway on a north landing or a few hundred feet before the taxiway on a south landing. (That is for light airplanes; in a twin the point would be much sooner.) If, after landing, it appeared that a stop wouldn't be possible, that would be tough. I'd just stay down and go on off the end.

The hazard in a late go-around is precisely the same as the hazard in a marginal takeoff with a strong crosswind, as covered in the discussion of wind effects on the departure phase of flight.

SHEARED ON APPROACH

Wind shear is an approach hazard that we all need to understand. The most common shear problem is created by a decreasing headwind component on final. It is not uncommon to find strong winds, thirty knots or more, at 1,000 or 2,000 feet with the wind nearly calm at the surface. As the airplane descends, it is not in a steady wind and the airspeed will be affected.

Wind shear effect on airspeed is a bit hard to grasp, with

perhaps the best rationalization coming from a comparison of groundspeed and airspeed. If the airspeed is ninety knots on final and the airplane is flying with a thirty-knot headwind as it descends through 1,000 feet, the groundspeed will be sixty knots. Simple. Now shear means the wind abruptly changes direction or velocity—with altitude in this example. Imagine that the wind drops to almost zero at 500 feet. As the airplane continues its descent from 1,000 feet, the airspeed remains on ninety and the groundspeed stays at sixty. Then the airplane moves rather quickly into the level where the wind is calm. At that level, the groundspeed would become ninety knots, the same as the airspeed, right? Right, but not immediately. The airplane's groundspeed was sixty knots as it descended from the thirty-knot headwind into the calm wind, and there's no way the airplane can instantly accelerate thirty knots. Instead, the airspeed decays to try and match the groundspeed.

Light airplanes accelerate rapidly in such a situation, and you'd certainly not see a full thirty-knot sag in airspeed. The encounter is usually felt as somewhat of a sinking spell, with a drop in airspeed noted. The seat of our pants tells us to add power to arrest the sink rate and help the decaying airspeed. This usually suffices. (In heavy airplanes, especially jets, acceleration is slower and wind shear can have much more serious consequences.)

Reverse the situation and fly with a diminishing tailwind. There the airspeed will tend to build, and the airplane will feel almost buoyant. Using the values in the preceding example, except changing the thirty-knot headwind to a thirty-knot tailwind, the groundspeed would be 120 knots as the airplane descends into the calm wind and the airspeed would

try to match that momentarily. This sounds like free beer—
nothing to worry about—but it can also create a hazard, an
overshoot.

EXAMPLE

An ILS approach at Sioux Falls, S.D., one winter day
stands out as a prime example of the decreasing tailwind.
The ILS there is to the northeast. The wind 2,000 feet
above the ground was westerly and very strong, probably
around thirty-five knots. From the outer marker to the
runway the strong tailwind component would turn into a
crosswind because the surface wind was southeasterly and
rather fresh.

As I descended, my Skyhawk just did not want to stay on
the glide slope. It was trending high, and for quite a while,
perhaps as long as thirty seconds, I had the power off and
was tracking the glide slope at a rather high airspeed. It was
quite turbulent in clouds, too, another characteristic of
wind shear.

Such a situation creates its problem after the airplane
moves into the new wind situation. As the wind was changing and the airplane was adapting to the new situation, I
was just about in a power-off dive. At some point, that
would have to change back to a normal approach. That's
no problem in a Skyhawk if anticipated—change the pitch
attitude, add some power, and presto, everything is okay.
In a heavier airplane, though, it would be possible to bomb
right through the glide slope and into the ground if the

changing situation were not anticipated. It is interesting, I think, that in quite a number of premature arrivals by air carrier aircraft the airplane was initially high on the glide slope. A correction was made to return the aircraft to the glide slope, but the correction was either excessive or flown for too long and the aircraft descended through the glide slope and into the ground.

HOW?

How do we know of wind shear so that we might make allowance for it? Beware of any situation where there is a marked difference in surface wind and wind aloft. And watch it when operating in a frontal zone or when flying in the vicinity of a thunderstorm. These are the situations most likely to create classic wind shear situations. Any strong and gusty wind condition can create localized wind shear that will affect the airplane momentarily.

The air carrier accidents related to wind shear are well documented. Airliners fly with flight recorders that show changes in airspeed as well as g-forces and other values. There is more guesswork to general aviation accidents, and there are probably a number of accidents in which wind shear is at least a contributing factor but isn't mentioned in the accident report because the investigators don't really have any after-the-fact means to pinpoint the possibility.

Wind, be it steady, gusty, or of the shear variety, is something to respect but not to fear. It affects takeoff performance, bounces the airplane around, and can induce variations to the approach and landing that we'd perhaps rather do without. Any reasonable wind-related risk is manageable, though. A pilot must only stay proficient at flying in wind, anticipate the effects, and fly with a cool head.

5 | The Stall/Spin

Back in the good old days, when airplanes were toys and the stall and cruising speeds were within a breath of one another, the stall/spin accident reigned supreme. Then came faster airplanes that were truly useful for flying across the country. The travel capability of these machines quickly outstripped the weather capability of pilots, and weather-related accidents moved to the forefront. In recent years, though, the pendulum seems to be swinging back a bit toward the stall/spin.

One positive note can be related to this. The accident rate has been improving slowly and steadily, and if the stall/spin has become a larger proportion of the total, that means something else is showing marked improvement. This would have to be in the weather area—a direct result of more pilots moving into IFR operations.

The stall/spin accident is deceptively simple. It involves

only the pilot not letting the airplane fly. It can thus be subjected to black-and-white discussion. Stalls are not like weather, where the go/no-go decision can be as fuzzy around the edges as early morning fog. They are not like night flying, where it can be technically VFR but practically IFR. And they are not like wind, where you might have a self-imposed wind limit of thirty knots and have to rationalize a situation where it's twenty-five gusting to thirty-five. A stall is a stall. The airplane is or is not in a stalled condition. And if provoked into a spin, there is no doubt about that condition of flight, no doubt at all.

PET THEORIES

There are plenty of pet theories on stall/spin accidents. Some students of the subject feel that most happen as the pilot makes the last turn in the pattern, from base to final. Others cite the departure phase of flight, especially from short fields. And a bunch of stall/spin accidents happen as the pilot maneuvers after a power failure. Those areas *are* strong factors, but something else is very high on the list. A substantial number of stall/spin accidents occur away from the airport, with the airplane functioning normally in a mechanical sense but with the pilot malfunctioning, or at least behaving foolishly. Buzzing, low-level aerobatics and low passes are real killers. Figure 4 shows that in a one-year period, such aerial exhibitionism was the number two factor in stall/spin accidents, second only to problems in the initial climb segment of flight.

BUZZING

In studying stall/spin accidents that occur when pilots become playful, plenty of similarities develop. The people involved tend to be students or relatively inexperienced private pilots. The airplanes are of the variety most often used for training. This is logical. There is no way a new pilot can take the airplane home to show the neighbors—no way, that is, other than through the medium of low-altitude flight. The temptation to do this is often strong—and fatal. Some buzzing accidents do involve more experienced pilots, and when this is the case, the buzz job is usually embellished with low-level aerobatics.

A buzzing accident is rather easy to dismiss: The pilot let his ego take command and he busted his tail. No sympathy can be generated for anyone other than passengers and survivors in such a case. The element of risk is obvious; the pilot elects to take the risk and then can't handle it. Of far more interest is the stall/spin that occurs as a pilot is flying normally, or at least as the pilot is operating within the framework of the rules.

TRAINING FLIGHTS

A few spin to the ground during training flights. These are usually solo flights, the purpose of which was stall practice. The scenario is logical: A student pulls the airplane up into

Figure 4. Fatal stall/spin accidents. One year.

| Initial climb | | Buzzing, low-level aerobatics | | After engine failure | | Landing pattern | | Low-altitude circling | | Go-around | | Practice stalls, intentional spins | |
TWIN	SNGL	TWIN	SNGL	TWIN	SNGL	TWIN	SNGL	TWIN	SNGL	TWIN	SNGL	TWIN	SNGL
	AA5A												
	AA5A												
	BE23												
	BE35												
	BE35												
	BL7A		AA1A										
	BL7A		AA1C										
	BL7E		ARC3										
	BL7G		BE19										
	BL7G		BE19										
	BL8G		BE24										
	BL14		BE35										
	C150		BL7A										
	C150		BL7A		BE24								
	C150		BL7D		BE35								
	C152		BL7E		BE35								
	C172		BL7K		BE35								
	C172		BL7K		BL14								
	C180		BL7K		C150								
	C182		BL8G		C150								
	C182		BL8K		C170								
	C185		BL8K		C182								
	C206		BL8K		HBLT								
	DHC3		C150		HBLT								
	HBLT		C150		HBLT				BE35				
	LLA4		C150		HBLT		AA1B		BL7A				
	LUS8		C150		MO20		BE35		BL7G				
	MAU4		C150		PA16		BE35		BL7K				
	MO20		C150		PA22		C172		BL7K				
	MO20		C150		PA24		C182		BL8G				
	PAJ3		C172		PA28		BL14		C152				
	PA14		C172		PA28		GLKS		C170				
	PA18		C172		PA28		MO20		C172		BE23		
	PA18		C172		PA28		PA18		C172		BE35		
	PA24		C172		PFLD	BE18	PA18		C182		C150		BE19
	PA28		HBLT	BE18	PT17	BE55	PA24		C305		C150		BL7A
	PA28		PS2A	C310	R114	BE58	PA28		MO20		C150		C150
	PA28		PAJ3	MTU2	TCFT	BE95	PA28		PA18		PA12		HBLT
	PA28		PAJ3	PA30	TCFT	C411	PA32		PA20		PA28		PA18
BE18	PA32		PAJ3	PA31	TCFT	LJ23	PA32		PA28		PA32		PA28
C421	P51D	None	TCFT	R690	WACO	PA23	TCFT	None	PA28	BE18	PA32	None	R112

a stall, mishandles it at the stall, spins the airplane, and then does not do the proper things to recover from the spin. In most cases, the airplane is one that is certified for spins, so recovery should have been no problem. We will explore that later.

There are also some stall/spin training accidents involving instructors. For the most part, these involve airplanes that are not certificated for spins but that are spun for one reason or another. Certainly it is foolish to intentionally spin an airplane that isn't certificated for the maneuver because the reason spins aren't approved is usually related to poor recovery characteristics. That is more than enough reason not to spin one just for kicks. The rules basically say that in single-engine airplanes not certificated for spins the manufacturer must demonstrate recovery from a one-turn spin in not more than one additional turn. There is no spin requirement for the certification of light twins. Anyone who spins past one turn in a single that isn't certificated for spins or spins a twin at all has suddenly assumed the role of experimental test pilot. No experimental test pilot would spin such an airplane at all without a parachute and a quick release door on the airplane. Most would also want a spin chute at the tail of the airplane to facilitate recovery from a flat spin.

OTHER REASONS

Some pilots spin-in away from the airport for other reasons. In a sample of accidents, a twin had an engine failure while

IFR and was subsequently seen spinning out of the bottom of the clouds. Two engines didn't do that pilot much good. The entire twin question will be discussed in Chapter 8, but this is an example of the problems caused by a combination of asymmetric thrust and a stall. There are also numerous stall/spin accidents after the engine fails in a single. Figure 4 shows this to be a relatively large part of the total picture. We'll explore it more in Chapter 8, but here we should at least consider that the record shows poor pilot performance in this area. This makes forced landings a lot more serious than they need to be. It's pure conjecture, but I'd be willing to bet that if the pilots had kept the airplanes flying until they contacted the ground or the trees, a very substantial percentage of those engine failure accidents would not have been fatal. It's pretty simple: when the airplane is stalled, it hits with a very high sink rate, often nose down. The sudden stop is survivable only in airplanes with very low stalling speeds, and then it's marginally survivable. On the other hand, if the airplane is flown into the ground or the trees, still under control, the rate of sink is survivable and deceleration in the horizontal becomes the question. The chances of avoiding a direct hit on something as hard as the ground are good, so in almost all cases the deceleration will be gentler than when hitting the ground while stalled, or in a spin.

You might say that avoiding a stall/spin is one of the most important items of technique on a forced landing because the stall/spin is the one thing most likely to spell disaster. It should be mentioned that the engine failures represented in Figure 4 are from all causes, including fuel starvation and exhaustion.

There are a lot of stall/spin accidents around the airport. In most every case, extenuating circumstances nudge the pilot along toward trouble.

The greatest number of stall/spin accidents came in initial climb during the year covered by Figure 4. This does not mean that pilots stall airplanes in normal climbs. Nor does this represent engine failures on takeoff. Those are included in the engine failure column. It does indicate that we do very poorly in managing risks, in avoiding the things that cause problems in initial climb. These accidents are most often related to overloading, high-density altitudes, high terrain near the airport, short strips, or to any combination of those things. Any one of these things can be a setup for a stall/spin accident; make it more than one, and an accident moves toward the "sure thing" category.

There are a substantial number of stall/spin accidents on approach. Some come in the turn from base to final, especially where lining up with the runway is made difficult because of a non-standard pattern, or because a downwind condition on base leg causes an overshoot of the turn to final. Horsing around leads to some problems in the pattern as pilots make steep turns a part of maneuvering for landing. And as we study stall/spin accidents, one thing stands out regardless of the phase of flight: the unintentional stall that leads to a serious problem is much more likely in turning than in level flight.

FLAPS

It is possible to link some stall/spin accidents to flaps or to the pilot's misunderstanding of the flaps. A go-around is the most likely place to find trouble because of this. Some airplanes will just barely fly level with full flaps, even at full power, so there is an apparent need to retract flaps early in a go-around. Retraction of flaps raises the stalling speed, though, and this must be recognized when retracting flaps in a tedious situation. A lot of simulated go-around drill during training or checkout is good preventive action. The trim changes that accompany the retraction of flaps can then be anticipated when the chips are down, as can the effect of flaps on stalling speed or lift. On a Skyhawk, for example, the first ten degrees of flaps lowers the stalling speed by almost five knots. Going from ten degrees onto full forty degrees of flaps lowers the stalling speed only an additional three knots. In a pinch you would be getting rid of a lot of drag while accepting a small increase in stalling speed by retracting flaps from forty to ten degrees, but in retracting from ten to zero, it would be a matter of increasing the stalling speed quite a bit for a slight decrease in drag. The situation is different on other airplanes; the straight information is in the pilot's operating handbook. And seeing, feeling and exploring the effects of flaps retraction should be part of every checkout.

IT'S LOGICAL

The factors found in stall/spin accidents, whether they happen around or away from airports, are logical enough. We can study the times, places, and circumstances and say, "Yes, old Joe spun in because. . . ." We know that the stalling speed increases with angle of bank, for example, and the relationship between this and stall/spin accidents is made clear by the fact that accidental spins often start in turns. What is not logical is the lack of pilot discipline involved in such accidents. Surely every pilot is aware of the seriousness of flying in a manner that increases the risk of a stall at low altitude or of a spin that flattens into an unrecoverable mode or of arrival at the ground in any kind of spin. Every pilot is aware of how you stall an airplane. There's no way to do it without increasing the wing's angle of attack to the stalling angle. By the same token, a reduction in angle of attack will, if done at the proper time, preclude a stall or entry into a spin.

POOR PORTRAYAL

My opinion is that what is taught in training today does not always portray the stall/spin problem as it exists. For example, in stall recovery the emphasis is on putting the nose on the horizon and applying full power. This often works quite well, but it is not always realistic. Why? Because power (or additional power) is not available in a high percentage of the situations that lead to stall/spin accidents. In departure and go-around accidents the engine is generally operating at full power to begin with. There is no way to add power. If the problem is engine failure on takeoff for whatever reason, we have no power to add. The buzzing stall/spin accidents generally come with the engine roaring —you sure don't buzz to be quiet. Some of the spins in training can be related to not reducing power instead of not applying it. (Cutting the power is a prime requirement in spin recovery in most airplanes.) The only place where the use of power might really help is in moving away from the stall on a normal approach.

REDUCE ANGLE OF ATTACK

Might it not be better to develop a strong understanding of angle of attack and think in terms of reducing angle of attack—wheel or stick forward—as *the* means of stall recovery or avoidance? Power, if available, can be used as a secondary item to help the airspeed move up and to minimize altitude loss. But if the mind is to be charged with a useful, all-purpose plan in case of trouble, it would have to be related to angle-of-attack reduction with the elevator—something that is always available.

THE ANGLE

Angle of attack is the single most important thing to understand when contemplating the stall/spin accident. What is angle of attack? It is basically the difference between where the wing is pointed and where the wing is going. At cruise the wing is about level and the airplane is going ahead; the angle is very small. Pull the nose up to a thirty-degree angle above the horizon, and initially the angle of attack remains small as the airplane zooms upward, climbing and dissipating speed. As the airplane slows, the angle of attack starts increasing rapidly if you hold the nose at that thirty-degree angle. The increase can be seen by comparing the vertical speed indication with the nose-up pitch attitude. When the nose is first pulled up, there is a lot of rate of climb: The airplane is pointed up and it is going up. Then the rate of climb begins decaying even though the nose is held high. That is evidence of increasing angle of attack. The vertical speed will be down close to zero as the airplane stalls.

ZOOM

In a buzzing accident a pilot might pull into such a thirty-degree nose-up attitude in a last and dramatic zoom. Or the nose might be pulled higher than thirty degrees above the horizon. Speed dissipates, and by the time it's down to a value that might alarm the pilot, the airplane could be more or less committed to disaster. The pilot might look at the airspeed and see it on a reasonable value when well into the zoom, giving a false feeling of well-being. The angle of attack might be increasing so rapidly at that point, though, that it will reach the stalling angle even after the pilot begins to reduce back pressure in an effort to reduce angle of attack. If the pilot had mentally compared the nose-up pitch angle with the full power stalling angle, though, the pilot would have noted that the difference exceeded the stalling angle of attack—a sure indication of impending trouble.

THE INSIDIOUS STALL

Such an ending is reserved for those who buzz. Of more concern is the insidious stall, the one that bites a pilot who is trying to maneuver an airplane for a purpose: to get over, around, or safely down. The part about angle of attack is equally important here, but it is more difficult to see.

Set the stage with a descending left turn. As the airplane is banked, back pressure must be held on the stick or wheel to keep the nose from dropping. A little is fine, but recognize a message: The nose wants to be lower in a turn because the airplane is trying to seek the same angle of attack it was trimmed for in level flight. The airplane is trying to protect itself. By adding back pressure, the pilot is increasing the angle of attack, cutting the margin between the actual and the stalling angle. As you hold back pressure in a turn, you are resisting the airplane's desire to protect itself (and you). In normal turns this is a necessary action if altitude is to be maintained, and it is perfectly safe. It's a different matter when low and slow.

Now we are in a thirty-degree banked descending turn. Drag increases as g-load builds and angle of attack increases. The rate of descent will increase. The eye might perceive this increased closure rate with the ground as being undesirable and send a message to the brain to do something about it. If the brain suffers from the illusion that the elevator control is an absolute controller of up and down, of altitude, the solution might be to add some more back pressure.

TURN FASTER

Meanwhile, perhaps the turn is not progressing satisfactorily. How do you make the airplane turn faster? More bank, which will further decrease the gap between actual and the stalling angle of attack, or a touch of rudder to skid the airplane around to the new heading a bit more swiftly. Choose rudder? Carry on—it helps promote the type of problem we are discussing.

The addition of rudder in the direction of turn tends to make the airplane want to bank more steeply. It is called *overbanking,* and the obvious solution is a bit of aileron in the opposite direction, to the right in case of our left turn.

The stage is almost set, so pause for a moment to reflect on the basic cause of a spin. One wing stalls while the other one is flying and becomes more deeply stalled than the other wing as things progress. Yaw is the best medium for this. What better way to generate yaw at the stall than a skidding turn? In our case, the right wing is flying faster than the left wing. The left wing's angle of attack is at 16.5 degrees now; the right isn't so precariously near the stall.

All the controls are still working to some extent as the turn continues. Pull back on the wheel a little more in a misguided attempt to arrest the rate of sink. A little more left rudder to speed the turn. And a little more right aileron to combat the overbanking. The rate of sink increases more, and the bank suddenly steepens precipitously. The time has come. The left wing reaches its stalling angle of attack and gives up. The right wing is still playful and keeps trying to fly.

The event develops into a spin from the bottom of a turn. The airplane spins to the left from a left turn. This is a rather sudden maneuver in most airplanes, one in which the airplane goes vertical or even slightly inverted as it falls off into the spin. Even if recovery is instituted immediately, a substantial amount of altitude will likely be lost. If it happens low to the ground, someone's nose is going to be muddied.

THE KEYS

A lot of things warn when this is about to happen. One key is back pressure. The pilot is pulling back on the wheel, no doubt about that. Too much pull should be a warning. The opposite aileron to combat overbanking should be a warn-

ing, too. Anytime it takes a considerable amount of opposite aileron to keep the airplane from exceeding the desired
angle of bank it is time to reduce the angle of attack. It is
also time to check the slip and skid indicator (ball), because it'll probably tell the tale on skid in the direction of
bank—a suggestion that you get your foot off the bottom
rudder.

A spin from the bottom of a turn would most likely come
as the airplane is being maneuvered for landing, or as it is
being turned at low altitude immediately after takeoff or for
the purpose of circling something on the ground.

MIRAGE

The visual illusion in a power-off, or low-power approach,
might be one of already having the nose down below the
horizon. Thus, putting the nose on the horizon and adding
power for recovery would not be applicable, as you'd have
to increase angle of attack to accomplish that. Angle of
attack can be at the stalling level even with the nose down;
all it takes is the difference between where the wing is
pointed and where it is going. This is most pronounced in
turns.

IN THE BEGINNING

Even during initial climb, the nose is not likely very high as
the airplane approaches a problem. When we practice stalls
at altitude, the approach to the stall is from an airspeed

above the stall. The nose is high because we had to put it there to dissipate speed. In a departure situation the approach to the stall is from a low airspeed, and as often as not the problem is in failing to obtain airspeed rather than failing to maintain it.

ELUSIVE HORIZON

The horizon is often elusive during departure. The tops of trees ahead do not likely represent the horizon, and if the terrain slopes upward or there is a mountain in the distance, the horizon can be difficult, if not impossible, to determine. In such a situation, what you feel and what you see on the instrument panel in the way of attitude and airspeed indications must be the governing factors. If there is doubt about getting over the trees or clearing an obstruction, pulling back on the wheel to make a staggering airplane go up is just not the ticket.

AILERONS

The role of the ailerons in stall/spin accidents must be further contemplated because the improper use of ailerons in some airplanes can actually lead to a spin—even with the rudder centered. And the role of ailerons is directly related to difficulty in spin recovery by a pilot not familiar with spins.

As noted, yaw at the moment of stall is what makes an airplane spin. Some airplanes tend to stall and fall through straight ahead; others don't. When one doesn't, the cause is either poor rigging or just the basic design of the airplane. If the ailerons alone are used in an attempt to keep the wings level in a stall or to keep the airplane from overbanking as it reaches the stall in a turn, some airplanes can be provoked to spin simply by that use of ailerons as the airplane stalls.

ADVERSE YAW

Remember adverse yaw? For example, move the wheel to the right and note that the nose of the aircraft swings a bit to the left as it rolls into a right turn. There is more drag on the lowered aileron than on the raised one. That phenomenon is more pronounced at the stall, as the flow separates from the top of the wing and the upward deflected aileron loses its bite. So if the airplane rolls to the left at the stall and you apply full right aileron, the effect will be to intensify the yaw to the left. The lowered left aileron does it. The lowered aileron also serves the purpose of demanding that wing to generate some lift to come back to level. That also promotes the stall. More up than down aileron travel minimizes this on most airplanes. The spinproof Ercoupe of a few decades ago had the ultimate aileron guard against the spin: Its roll control was virtually accomplished with up aileron only. When the wheel was full right, for example, the right aileron would be all the way up and the left one almost flush.

NEW WORLD

Once in an aileron-induced spin, a pilot is in a strange new world. The entry into a spin is quick and disorienting. A pilot's first thought is related to what is going on; many pilots do not realize it is a spin. Rather, they think something is basically wrong with the flying machine. The control wheel might be full back and to the right, yet the airplane is pointed straight down and is rotating to the left. The correct recovery procedure for most airplanes is to neutralize the wheel, in both roll and pitch. If that is done quickly, it's probably enough; the airplane will at that moment make the transition from spin to dive. If this fails to stop the spin, rudder would be required to stop the rotation as the wheel is moved to a neutral position. But it is not easy to move the wheel forward and to the left when the airplane is going madly down and to the left. That is why some student pilots spin all the way to the ground from a respectable altitude after accidentally spinning an airplane. The proper recovery action is so unnatural that their minds simply can't make the hands do the necessary work. And even when a recovery is instituted promptly, almost 1,000 feet can be lost in a spin, especially one from the bottom of a turn.

Spin recovery problems can also come when a pilot fails to close the throttle in an accidental spin. Power tends to make a spin flatten, and once an airplane is in a flat spin the sure method of recovery becomes parachute-related.

SOLUTIONS

It is easier to find fault with today's methods of stall practice than it is to suggest great new ways to look at the
problem. The only realistic way to simulate the insidious
stall at low altitude would be to do stalls at low altitude.
That would create more problems than it might solve. The
real solutions are probably in individual understanding of
the situations in which stall/spin accidents occur—critical
initial climb situations—buzzing, unwarranted low flying,
and anything that leads to low and slow turns—and avoidance of those things. The indications of an impending problem should be mentally filed for reference, too. The portents
of trouble are a lot of back pressure held on the wheel or a
lot of aileron against a turn. Rapidly decaying airspeed is
also a warning, as is a substantial angular difference between
where the airplane is pointed and where it will really go
with the power selected. These are all things to understand
and be wary of.

Another important item is the use of rudder. Back in the
good old days, it was taught that the rudder is the one
control that is effective through the stall. Rudder controls
yaw, so the rudder and the rudder alone can be used to
keep the airplane from spinning as the airplane stalls. This
was often demonstrated in what was called a "complete"
stall. The drill was to stall the airplane and keep it stalled,
keeping the wheel or stick full aft until the nose dropped
through the horizon. The aileron would remain centered,

and the rudder would be used to keep the wings level. It was good exercise and a good demonstration. The airplanes of the day (Cubs, Aeroncas, and the like) were good spinners and would often reward a poor effort with a spin. Also, for the pilot who didn't believe that ailerons could cause an airplane to spin, a convincer was to keep the stick back and the airplane stalled while trying to keep the wings level with the ailerons instead of with the rudder. Got a lot of spins out of that.

IN YOUR HAND

Foremost, though, is an understanding of what the elevators of an airplane really do. They control angle of attack, not up and down, not altitude. Many accidental spins are probably related to a strong notion that the elevators control altitude—pull back to go up. That doesn't work when the chips are down. Angle of attack is the key to the stall, and the elevators are the key to angle of attack. Always think in terms of reducing angle of attack: wheel or stick forward when the airplane begins feeling squirrelly.

SPIN LESSON?

The increasing incident of stall/spin accidents has rekindled the controversy over whether or not spins should be demonstrated or taught to all pilots. Certainly it can be argued that spin training might help in the instances where a student spins an airplane at altitude and never recovers. And it has always seemed a good idea at least to demonstrate spins to pilots flying airplanes that are easily spinnable.

But if we are to have a requirement for spins then the airplane builders will be forced to build airplanes that are easy to spin. If they are easy to spin intentionally, they might also be easy to spin accidentally. This might be counterproductive. The best thing to do in relation to spinning would be to build airplanes that are difficult to spin—accidentally or on purpose.

6 | A Weighty Subject

The morning paper said only that the airplane had crashed while taking off, and that two people were dead and two critically injured. No details. It happened at a friend's airport—a rather small grass strip—and I started to call him but decided against it. He might be busy, and I could find out more later. As I was thinking about it, he telephoned to ask me to come have a look and talk with him about the accident. It made two of a kind at his airport (over a long period of time), and he was concerned.

The airstrip is 2,200 feet long, grass, manicured like a golf green, and it was resplendent in sparkling sunshine as I rounded the bend in the river to land downwind. The approaches are better that way, and it would take at least ten knots of wind to urge an upwind landing from over the obstructions. The accident of the day before happened as the pilot took off toward those obstructions with four people in a four-place airplane. The airport is well within the capability of most light airplanes (I've seen a King Air use it with no problems), but it is a field that requires care and thought. Certainly there is nothing wrong with this. Not every runway in the land can be 5,000 feet long with clear approaches.

After I landed, the airport owner told me about the accident. The FAA and NTSB people had already done their work and left. There were enough facts and there had been enough witnesses, all with about the same observations, for the Feds to write the accident up and go away.

OVER GROSS

In addition to having four men and 183 pounds of baggage on board, the pilot elected to fill the fuel tanks. The investigators computed the actual takeoff weight to be approximately 200 pounds over gross. If all the baggage was in the baggage compartment, the center of gravity would have been outside the aft limits. The airplane manual suggests the use of flaps for short field takeoffs, but witnesses reported that flaps were not used. There was a gusty crosswind.

The airplane must have become airborne about two-thirds of the way down the runway. Almost immediately after lift-off, the pilot apparently elected to abort the takeoff. The visual picture at such a point would have suggested a very difficult situation at best if the airplane was not flying eagerly.

Witnesses did not agree on where the airplane touched back down, and the only tire marks in the grass were a few hundred feet past the official end of the runway, still on level and smooth turf but very near the rough. The airplane was still on runway heading as it passed near a house and moved between two trees, shearing both wing tips. The next obstructions were much less friendly. Reacting to the upcoming trees and deep gully, the pilot must have pulled the wheel back because it appeared that the airplane struck two very substantial trees while about five or six feet in the air in quite a nose-high attitude. One tree got the left wing about a third of the way out toward the tip. The left side of the nose struck the other tree: There was wood imbedded in the left front cylinder, and pieces of engine baffle were imbedded in the tree.

The airplane was probably moving at from fifty to sixty knots at impact. The left wing stopped at the tree, but its gas tank was flung to the other side of the gully. Some part of the left front side of the fuselage stopped, but the heavy parts continued on. The instrument panel was down in the gully, the engine was on the other side, and the nose gear was beyond the engine. The right wing was down in the gully, and the cabin door and the floor of the forward cabin were still loosely attached to the right wing. The right front seat was still on the floor by the door. The forward fuselage was completely shattered, but the aft fuselage, from about two-thirds of the way back in the cabin, stopped at the trees and remained relatively intact. The rear seats did not stay in place as the cabin floor came apart. The baggage and the people came to rest down in the gully. The survivors were in the rear seats.

THOUGHT-PROVOKING

Accident sites are both sad and thought-provoking. The thought of an airplane being transformed into such a mess in a split second is difficult to accept. The thought that people lost their lives as it happened is unhappy at best. And the concept of an intelligent and successful person stacking the unfavorable odds by overloading an airplane on a relatively small airport is one of the perplexing, recurring, and hard-to-understand phenomena of general aviation.

With full fuel the flight would have been nonstop to home base. This must have had some bearing on the pilot's decision to fill it up. Nobody knows why the pilot did not select takeoff flaps or why the runway with the worst obstructions was selected.

A lesson, a tragic lesson. Some might point a finger at the beautiful airstrip—idyllic, waiting for people to realize the true potential of an airplane by flying to where they want to go. Some might point a finger at the little airplane; it killed, it is a villain. Not true. What is true is that the airstrip, and airplanes in general, are unforgiving of many types of basic errors. Meanwhile, the trees survive, growing slowly and patiently. The pieces of metal imbedded in the trunk will probably stay there. If a pilot tempted with overloading would only look at that tree before doing so, it would teach a lesson silently, painlessly, and at no cost. If the lesson couldn't be learned the easy way, the tree stands ready to teach it the hard way, again and again.

NTSB REPORT

In a pamphlet discussing weight and balance as a safety consideration, the National Transportation Safety Board notes 213 related accidents in the U.S. during a five-year period. The 213 accidents resulted in 273 fatalities and 115 serious injuries, which underlines the fact that these accidents tend to be serious when they do occur. The NTSB report gave a number of examples, and it is noteworthy that in virtually every case at least one other factor combined with the overload or imbalance to make a difficult situation impossible, as was the case in the accident just described. One pilot attempted takeoff in an overloaded airplane at a density altitude of 9,800 feet. Another overloaded his airplane and crashed while attempting an uphill takeoff at a density altitude of 3,000 feet. A light airplane that was 244 pounds over gross crashed while attempting a takeoff on a very hot day. A twin crashed shortly after encountering icing conditions following an overweight takeoff.

CG

Those were primarily related to weight; there are numerous accidents with center-of-gravity connections, too.

When trouble comes, the center of gravity is usually aft of the limit, and the flight usually ends in a stall/spin because this condition affects the longitudinal stability of an airplane. In severe cases of aft CG, the nose of an airplane pitches up and continues up until the airplane stalls, even though the pilot applies full forward elevator—a very unpleasant thought.

Of the two limitations, weight and CG, weight offers the most temptations. Rare is the airplane that can carry full fuel, full seats, and full baggage. And while most users seldom have need to do all those things simultaneously, the need does occasionally arise to extract that much utility from the airplane. Ironically, that need seems to present itself on smaller airports more often than not. The smaller airports tend to be used more during recreational flights, when the load factor is highest. Take as many people as possible to the fun spot, and don't leave any gear behind. To compound the problem, add the heat of summer, when recreational flying is at its peak, to prolong the takeoff run and cut the rate of climb.

RATE OF CLIMB

Next, consider that rate of climb is the item which most often sets the gross weight limit of light airplanes. The regulations require that an airplane climb at sea level, in standard conditions, 11.5 times the stalling speed (in knots) with takeoff power, the gear extended in the case of a retractable, and with takeoff flaps. The fact that rate of climb is the airplane's tender spot in relation to weight makes it logical that most accidents involving overloaded airplanes happen during initial climb.

For example, consider a 150-horsepower Cessna Sky-hawk with a 230-pound (10 percent) overload condition on a ninety-degree day at 2,500 feet elevation. The airplane's normal rate of climb in standard conditions is 645 feet per minute. The temperature and elevation cuts that to 480 feet per minute. The overload slices that 480 down to 384 feet per minute. (The effect of overloading on perform-ance is twice the percentage over gross. In this example 10 percent over means 20 percent less climb.) The angle of climb speed increases to sixty-three knots, and the result is a rather flat climb. (Performance speeds—stall, climb, and maneuvering—change at a rate approximately half the per-centage over or under gross weight. For 10 percent over, add 5 percent to the climb speed in this example.) A downdraft or some turbulence might, in fact, make the rate of climb less than the amount necessary to climb one foot for each twenty feet of forward motion. That is rather critical because the obstruction criteria for VFR runways calls for a 20:1 slope. (All runways do not meet this slope requirement.)

In most weight-related accidents the pilot could in fact take the information in the aircraft manual and the rules of thumb just given to determine the effects of overloading and see on paper that the proposed mission is impossible. This is certainly a sensible precaution to take if there is any doubt.

STRUCTURE

An overload also compromises the airplane's structural strength, but this doesn't appear as the cause of great problems. I can't remember a single accident in which an over-loaded airplane failed when operated within airspeed limits, though there might have been some. There are instances of overloaded airplanes failing after the pilot lost control in adverse weather conditions, but in these instances the airplane would likely have broken regardless of the weight.

The reason airplanes don't break when overloaded is because they are quite strong. Again using a Skyhawk at 10 percent over gross as an example, the limit load factor drops only from 3.8 to 3.45 G's. That is a far less catastrophic change than the 20-percent increase in takeoff distance, 20-percent decrease in rate of climb, and greater-than-20-percent decrease in climb gradient. We almost never even get close to the limit load factor of an airplane, but on those hot and short strips we are often very close to situations where the maximum rate of climb is required to get the airplane up and over the obstacles.

DON'T MISUNDERSTAND

That is not meant to condone overloading when runway length isn't a consideration. Overloading does cut the structural margin, and thus it shouldn't be done. Another likely problem caused by an overload is engine overheating as the airplane struggles to lift the weight.

In a sense the pilot becomes an experimental test pilot when an airplane is overloaded because the airplane is being asked to perform outside the envelope it was subjected to in testing. Even so it is sometimes hard to argue with the pilot who overloads an airplane slightly to avoid a fuel problem at the end of a flight if the departure runway is long and surface temperatures are not high. The rationale in such a situation might be that the compromise in climb and structural strength will affect the safety of the flight only slightly, whereas a compromise in the fuel load will affect the safety of the flight substantially. It can be a tough decision, but the right answer has to be the legal answer: Pick an airplane that will fly legally with both the desired fuel and payload and stay within the weight limits.

There should be no temptation on exceeding the center-of-gravity limits of an airplane because controllability becomes the question with CG. There are no formulas to use in illustrating what exceeding the limit a given amount might cause. The aft limit is the critical one and must be considered an absolute. The forward CG limit is usually based on landing considerations. The airplane must have enough elevator effectiveness to land on the main wheels first at full-forward CG.

Spin recovery is one factor setting the aft CG limit on most single-engine airplanes. As noted, a single-engine airplane must recover from a one-turn spin in not more than one additional turn, and manufacturers have been known to lose experimental airplanes in spins as they attempt to move the CG limit aft. When it gets too far aft, the spin flattens before one turn is completed, the test pilot has to use his parachute, and the aft CG limit of the airplane is moved forward.

Longitudinal stability also deteriorates as the CG moves aft, and if the airplane is loaded far enough aft, the airplane ceases to have positive longitudinal stability. An airplane becomes difficult to fly when it reaches this point, where virtually no force on the wheel is required to change pitch attitude. In an extreme case the nose of the aircraft just pitches up, and up, and keeps on going up until the airplane stalls, even with the elevator control full forward.

EXAMPLES

Two examples illustrate the potential of aft CG operation.

A twin was taking off with the CG far aft, and as the gear retracted (moving the CG back even more because of aft retraction), the nose of the aircraft started to pitch up. The nose-up trend continued until the aircraft stalled. Might the pilot have salvaged things by putting the gear back down? It is possible.

In another, a pilot had flown an airplane extensively for a number of years on the same type of mission, with the CG slightly aft of the limit on almost all flights. The airplane always did require quite a bit of nose-down trim, but he had no problem until the trim tab control rod broke, making trim unavailable. The pilot reported that it was barely within his physical capability to keep the nose of the aircraft from pitching up into a stall. The return and landing was successful but touchy.

EXPERIENCE DOESN'T HELP

It is interesting that commercial and airline transport-rated pilots were involved in almost 60 percent of the weight-and-balance-related accidents in a four-year period. Perhaps this suggests that experience prompts a pilot to feel immune to the effects of excessive weight or of exceeding the center-of-gravity limits. Whatever, it proves once again that the laws of gravity and aerodynamics don't make exceptions based on pilot experience.

DENSITY ALTITUDE

High density altitude often figures in weight-related accidents. It is important to note also that density altitude can be a factor in accidents where weight and balance are within limits. Pilots of Part 25 aircraft, air carriers and bizjets for the most part, must calculate the distance required for every takeoff, and required performance parameters must be met for every takeoff. This often requires that the airplanes be flown from high and hot airports at weights below gross. We don't have to meet this requirement in most general aviation operations, and many pilots feel that as long as the gross weight is not exceeded, everything will be okay. This is an erroneous assumption. The situation often arises, especially in high and hot country, where the only safe weight is one below gross weight.

MOUNTAIN FLYING

Mountain flying is a separate subject, best learned through dual instruction from an experienced mountain instructor before tackling the Rockies in a light airplane. One thing does stand out in the accidents that flatlanders have in the mountains, though: Any problem usually stems either from a disregard of the effects of wind over the mountains and the rule of thumb to stay out of the mountains when the wind at ridge levels is forecast in excess of thirty knots or from density altitude problems.

Those of us who are used to flying where field elevations are below a couple of thousand feet need to rethink carefully our situation before takeoff at a high altitude airport, as well as before heading across high terrain. The airplane knows only density altitude. Just because the specs say the airplane's ceiling is 13,500 feet, that does not mean the airplane will climb to that altitude on the altimeter. If it is eighty-three degrees at the Leadville, Colorado, airport (elevation 9,927), your 13,500-foot service ceiling airplane would be at its service ceiling while resting on the runway because that's about what the density altitude would be under the existing conditions. The only way to fly would be to lighten the load. (The same thing is often true at short airports.)

By the same token, a pilot flying an airplane with a 13,500-foot service ceiling wouldn't stand a chance of making it across an 11,000-foot ridge on a hot day at gross weight because the density altitude of the ridge top might be above 13,500 feet.

High temperatures can have a profound influence on takeoff, climb, and service ceiling. Risk management must begin with careful calculations and continue throughout the flight with continuing calculations and no self-deception. For the takeoff a good rule is to require a runway length at least equal to the calculated distance to takeoff and climb to fifty feet. That gives some margin for error. Margin is very necessary because all takeoff figures are based on perfection, a maximum effort—full throttle before brake release, a new engine, standard conditions, a hard and level surface, and flawless flying technique. Factors are included to allow for things like grass and higher- (or lower-) than-standard temperatures and elevation, but there's nothing there to use in padding the number for an engine that's not as peppy as it used to be or for flying technique that's not exactly swift. We must add some for good measure, and the use of the "over fifty-foot" figure in setting the absolute minimum for actual runway length works well here. If obstructions are close to the end of the runway, an additional allowance would need to be made. In every case, it is good to off-load some fuel or cabin weight if there is any doubt.

The next thing would be to ascertain that the engine is indeed putting out an appropriate amount of power and to be satisfied with this either before releasing the brakes or very early in the takeoff run. If the airplane has a fixed-pitch prop, look at static rpm; with a constant speed check rpm and manifold pressure. Just the feel of initial acceleration can be a good indication in a familiar airplane, too.

Once the roll starts, it is wise to recognize that there is a point of no return on every takeoff. Up to that point, aborting the takeoff will cause no problem. Pull the power back, put on the brakes, and stop with the airplane and people in the same condition as at the start of the roll. Past that point the choice is between a successful flight and an accident. In studying reports on takeoff accidents from small airports, it is hard to believe that there wasn't usually strong doubt in the pilot's mind before the airplane passed the point of no return on the runway.

The farther a pilot goes past the point of no return on an impossible takeoff, the more serious the accident that follows. If an abort is attempted late, as in the example at the beginning of this chapter, the entry into the rough will be at high speed. If the pilot keeps trying, gets the airplane off, but strikes obstructions or stalls the airplane in an attempt to "make" it fly over obstructions, the consequences might also be very serious.

Again, the situation is very much in the hands of the pilot. The information is available to determine that a takeoff will or will not be successful. Hunches, wishes, eyeball estimates, and guesses don't count. It is cut and dried. The airplane has measurable performance, and the runway and obstructions are known quantities. And weight plays a key role.

FLYING TECHNIQUE

Even the flying technique involved in a takeoff is a methodical procedure that must be followed. In jet aircraft a careful determination of lift-off speed is made. We should do the same thing in light airplanes. Once the field length has been calculated as adequate, a plan for the takeoff would include the determination of the lift-off and the best angle-of-climb speeds. In a 1974 Skyhawk operating at gross weight, for example, the pilot's operating handbook calls for lifting the nosewheel at fifty-two knots and climbing at fifty-nine knots until obstacles are cleared. The performance figures are based on the use of those speeds. Make the calculations, fly the speeds with precision, and have confidence in the proceedings. If you don't make the calculations and guess at the proper speeds, what comes next is anybody's guess. A careful computation of weight, balance, and performance is as important to the safety of a flight as is the weather check and the preflight inspection.

7 | Midair Collisions

There is an old, true, and somewhat trite saying that a midair collision can spoil your whole day. And, the thought of a midair probably strikes more fear into the hearts of pilots and laymen than does the thought of any other aerial misadventure. Many pilots are even egotistical enough to profess aeronautical fear only of the midair. It is the one thing not completely under their control and is thus the only thing they fear might ever sneak up and bite. The layman's fear is of being in an airplane that is struck by another airplane, usually a small airplane that, in the mind of an airline passenger, "shouldn't be there." Then the fear is of falling from the sky in the crippled machine. It is this public fear that prompts Congress to appropriate billions a year for the purpose of air traffic control.

There is at least some basis for apprehension about midair collisions. Even in a year when there are no collisions involving air carriers, about 100 people, pilots and passengers, plus or minus twenty or thirty, are involved in midair collisions in the United States. That number appears small when compared with the over 2,000 people involved in weather-related accidents, but it must be considered significant because it couples with a basic human fear.

MANY SURVIVE

A myth to puncture quickly is the one about your being automatically wiped out if involved in a midair collision. In fact, 60 to 65 percent of the people who are involved in midair collisions survive. That doesn't advertise it as an appealing new outdoor sport, but it does add perspective. This number is almost equal to the percentage who survive weather-related accidents, some of which are relatively simple encounters with wind or density altitude, and it is in excess of the percentage of participants who survive stall/ spin accidents. The midair collision thus must be positioned as a general aviation accident type only about equal in severity, though not, of course, in frequency, to the two biggies, weather and stall/spin.

It is quite possible to minimize risk in this area, too, because midair collisions follow a familiar pattern year after year. Most collisions occur within five miles of an airport. That is quite logical. Airplanes congregate at airports, and if most midairs occurred somewhere else, it would be strange indeed.

Also logically, collisions just naturally often tend to involve airplanes engaged in the type of flying that occurs near airports. In a two-year collection of over 100 midair collision reports used for research material, about 70 percent of the airplanes were on training, pleasure, or personal flights. These types of flying account for 50 percent of the total flight hours, so some extra exposure to the midair collision hazard is clearly identified. If your flying doesn't stray far from the airport, extra effort is required to minimize the risk of collision.

Business and corporate flying, which is usually cross-country, is responsible for about one-third of the flight hours and only about 6 percent of the aircraft involved in midair collisions. There is less exposure so there is less risk. Special purpose flying that results in airplanes congregating in one spot or flying together accounts for a number of collisions. Figure 5 shows what airplanes were doing when they collided. Collisions in agricultural flying are not included.

HIGH WING OR LOW

Another myth to dispel is that high-wing airplanes have a greater involvement in midair collisions than low-wing airplanes. In a two-year period studied the percentage involvement of high-wing airplanes was only slightly larger than the percentage of the fleet that is high wing. That leaves the high-wing birds with a little disadvantage, but because the percentage of high-wing airplanes doing the type of flying

Normal cruise	Final approach	Formation flying	Landing pattern, circling	Climbing to cruise	En route descent	Formation flying	Glider tow
AA1B							
AA5A							
BE35							
BE36							
BL14	BE45						
C150	BL7G						
C150	C150						
C150	C150						
C150	C150						
C150	C150						
C150	C150						
C150	C150						
C150	C150						
C150	C170						
C150	C172						
C150	C172						
C172	C172						
C172	C172						
C172	C177						
C175	C402						
C177	C414						
C177	DHC2						
C182	LUS8						
HBLT	MO20						
PAJ3	PA18	BL7A					
PA18	PA24	BL7G					
PA22	PA28	BL8G					
PA22	PA28	BL14	C150	BE50			
PA22	PA28	C150	C150	C150	BE33	BL7G	
PA28	PA28	C150	C150	C180	BE35	GLKS	
PA28	PA28	C340	C182	C206	CI72	HBLT	
PA28	PA28	C421	CVAR	PA28	DHC6	HBLT	
PA28	PA28	PA16	PA24	PA28	PA28	HBLT	BL7G
PA28	PA32	TCFT	R690	PA28	PA31	HBLT	PA18

Figure 5. Total midair collisions. Two years.
(Agricultural and military aircraft, helicopters
and gliders are not listed. If the collision was between
one of those aircraft and one of the above, only the
general-use fixed-wing airplane is listed.)

in which the midair collision hazard is highest—training, pleasure, and personal flying—is likely greater than the percentage of the low-wing airplanes involved in this activity. The closeness of the high/low-wing involvement in collisions could even be interpreted as indicating an advantage for the high wing. Perhaps the obvious visual limitation of high-wing airplanes prompts pilots to work at minimizing the effects of blind spots.

There is also a direct relationship between the type of airplane and the number of collisions. Cessna 150's are most frequently involved. The Cessna 172 is in the fleet in roughly similar numbers, yet its involvement in midairs is much lower than the 150. That is easy to explain. Perhaps half the 172's flying hours are in the area of high risk, while the rest are out in the straight and level, away from airports. The PA-28, also widely used in training and pleasure flying, is involved in a significant number of collisions. No other aircraft type had a significant enough individual involvement in midair collisions to mention.

DENSITY v. COLLISIONS

A relationship between traffic density and collisions is suggested in California. California contains 12 percent of the airplanes and was the scene of 24 percent of the midair collisions in a two-year period. One might challenge the density theory with the fact that aircraft population per 1,000 square miles in California is lower than in Florida and Ohio and about the same as Illinois. However, California's airplane population is concentrated at a relatively small number of airports in metropolitan areas, and this concentration combines with mountainous terrain to greatly limit the amount of airspace that is used by light aircraft. The visibility is pretty grungy in some of the California metropolitan areas much of the time, too.

No other state shows a continuing year-to-year midair collision history that is much higher than average.

It is worthy of note that a study of seven years' worth of collisions by the MITRE Corporation might be interpreted as contradicting the California theory by showing that midair collisions at uncontrolled airports increased linearly with operations: When operations doubled, midair collisions doubled. On the just stated theory that traffic density increases hazard, it might have been more logical for collisions to triple with a doubling of operations. Perhaps, though, pilots rise to the occasion when they know they are operating at a busy uncontrolled airport, and California's problem might be more closely related to the compacting of en route VFR traffic into flyways dictated by terrain than to the state's busy airports.

Most of the general aviation operations are concentrated at a relatively small percentage of the uncontrolled airports, with two-thirds of the operations at 8 percent of the airports. It is thus fortunate and encouraging that the collision hazard seems to increase linearly with traffic. The fact that collisions are almost directly related to operations does concentrate the action at the airports where traffic is concentrated, and this in turn might make it appear that these airports have more than their share of collisions until the true record is examined.

AT CONTROLLED AIRPORTS

The increase in collisions with traffic is nonlinear at controlled airports. There, low-activity airports remain virtually collision-free, with the collisions increasing dramatically as VFR traffic at controlled airports increases. The increase in collisions with traffic at controlled airports underlines a basic problem. When a pilot feels there is control, he must not be as alert as when he is in a situation where it is clear that only his eyeball is protecting the tail. This must be why the operation of a tower doesn't reduce the true collision hazard. When only fatal midair collisions are considered, the rate at uncontrolled airports is not significantly higher than the rate at controlled airports. In fact, in one recent year there were more fatal midair collisions at controlled airports than at uncontrolled airports.

CONFIGURATION

As airplanes actually collide, the encounters more likely involve high wing v. high wing and high wing v. low wing airplanes. These two types of collisions accounted for over 60 percent of the total encounters. Low wing v. low wing was next, and in one period (not the one covered by Figure

5.) almost 10 percent of the midairs studied involved a helicopter and an airplane.

HELICOPTERS?

The helicopter situation makes some suggestions. Helicopters have excellent visibility, and their involvement supports the NTSB's continuing 100 percent pilot error classification for midair collisions. The NTSB does assign other visual causal factors such as dirty windshields and sun glare to midairs, but they are generally satisfied that one and usually both pilots had the opportunity to make a timely sighting of the other traffic and maneuver to avoid the other airplane. Even when flying in a helicopter's bubble, a pilot must make the effort to look for other aircraft.

Another thought is that helicopters move in a manner that is unpredictable to fixed-wing pilots, and this makes them hard to find and track. We have a lot of clues on where to look for fixed-wing airplanes around an airport, but where do you look for helicopters? The airplanes all use the runway, but the helicopters can use ramp areas and can come and go in any direction. And whereas it might be reasoned that helicopters are likely to tangle with fast airplanes that sneak up behind them, most helicopter collisions involve plain old light airplanes—airplanes that tend to frequent the same low-altitude airspace as the chopper.

HIGH PERFORMANCE v. SLOW

I think we all consider the possibility of a high performance airplane sneaking up on a light airplane from an unlikely spot. This does happen, but not too often. There is only an occasional strike by a jet. In some military jets accidents, it has appeared that the jet was intercepting the slower airplane, accidentally on purpose in one case, and that has been examined and hopefully remedied by the military.

Some feel it a minor miracle that there aren't more military v. civil midair collisions because of the low-level maneuvering done by the air force on practice missions. Put into context, though, the number of missions flown divides into the size of the country to stack the odds against such encounters.

SAN DIEGO

Where there are high v. low performance airplane collisions involving airliners and when the big airplane crashes disastrously after the collision, as at San Diego, there's a tremendous amount of publicity. This particular one, between a 727 and a 172, became a milestone on the way to an expanded air traffic control system as well. The moments leading up to the San Diego collision are worthy of study because there is good illustration of the weaknesses in "see and be seen", as well as of the difficulty pilots might have concentrating on the aircraft spotting process. The transcript of what was said in the cockpit gives us a unique insight into this. Consider the last few minutes of the conversation within the airliner cockpit of the airliner, and of pertinent air traffic control communications. Intercockpit conversation is in italics and communications between the aircraft and an airline ground station are omitted.

TIME: 0859:39

Second Officer: "Yeah." (*Sound of laughter in the background.*)

Approach Control: "PSA 182, additional traffic's, ah, 12 o'clock, three miles, just north of the field northeastbound, a Cessna 172 climbing VFR out of 1,400."

First Officer: "*Very nice.*"

Second Officer: "*He really broke up laughing, I said, so I'm late.*"

Off-duty Captain in the cockpit: "*Yesterday we took off out of San Francisco; we're supposed to go over to Bay approach, you know, and I switched 24.9, I guess, and I said, Bay departure, PSA five, a gal comes on and she says, this is Oakland tower, and I said, Oh I'm sorry about that. Then I hesitated and then I said, In a way, I'm not sorry, though (sound of laughter), that really broke her up.*"

First Officer: "Okay, we've got that other twelve."

Approach Control: "Cessna 7711 Golf, San Diego departure, radar contact, maintain VFR conditions at or below 3,500, fly heading 070, vector final approach course."

TIME: 0900:10

(*Sound of laughter.*)

Approach Control: "PSA 182, traffic's at 12 o'clock, three miles, out of 1,700."

First Officer: *"Got 'em."*

Captain: "Traffic in sight."

Approach Control: "Okay, sir, maintain visual separation, contact Lindbergh tower 133.3, have a nice day now."

First Officer: *"Flaps two."*

Captain: "Okay."

Captain: "Lindbergh, PSA 182 downwind."

Tower: "PSA 182, Lindbergh tower, ah, traffic 12 o'clock, one mile, a Cessna."

First Officer: *"Flaps five."*

Captain: *"Is that the one . . . looking at?"*

First Officer: *"Yeah, but I don't see him now."*

Captain: "Okay, we had it there a minute ago."

Tower: "182, Roger."

Captain: "I think he's pass . . . off to our right."

Tower: "Yeah."

Captain: *"He was right over here a minute ago."*

First Officer: *"Yeah."*

TIME: 0900:53

Tower: "How far are you going to take your downwind 182? Company traffic is waiting for departure."

Captain: "Ah, probably about three to four miles."

Tower: "Okay."

Tower: "PSA 207, taxi into position and hold."

PSA 207: "207, position and hold."

Tower: "PSA 182, cleared to land."

Captain: "182's cleared to land."

(Sound similar to door closing.)

First Officer: *"Are we clear of that Cessna?"*

Second Officer: *"Supposed to be."*

Captain: "*I guess.*"

(Sound of laughter.)

Off-duty Captain: "*I hope.*"

Captain: "*Oh yeah, before we turned downwind, I saw him about one o'clock, probably behind us now.*"

First Officer: "*Gear down.*"

(Sound of clicks and sound similar to gear extension.)

First Officer: "*There's one underneath.*"

First Officer: "*I was looking at that inbound there.*"

(Sound of thump similar to nose gear door closing.)

Captain: "*Whoop.*"

First Officer: "*Aghh.*"

TIME: 0901:47

(Sound of collision.)

Off-duty Captain: "*Oh ##&%##.*"

Captain: "*Easy baby, easy baby.*"

Unidentified: "*Yeah.*"

Captain: "*What have we got here?*"

First Officer: "*It's bad.*"

Captain: "*Huh?*"

First Officer: "*We're hit man, we are hit.*"

Captain: "Tower, we're going down, this is PSA."

Tower: "Okay, I'll call the equipment for you."

Unidentified: "*Whoo.*"

(Sound of stall warning.)

Captain: "This is it baby."

Unidentified: "*Bob.*"

Captain: "*Brace yourself.*"

Unidentified: "*Hey baby.*"

Unidentified: "*Ma, I love yah.*"

TIME: 0902:04.5

(Sound of cockpit voice recorder ceases, electrical power to recorder stops.)

The National Transportation Safety Board found that if the eyes of the airline pilots were located at the aircraft's design reference point, the Cessna would have been visible from 170 up to 10 seconds prior to the collision, or for the time from the beginning of the conversation presented here. It would have been difficult for the pilots in the 172 to see the 727; the Cessna was climbing and was hit from behind. The 727 was descending.

It's pertinent that the 727 crew said the Cessna was in sight, and then lost sight of the airplane. It was probably being viewed against the background of the city, there was little relative motion, and any pilot who says he can constantly track a light airplane against a city background is making a pretty fancy claim about his eyesight. It's difficult, very difficult. And in this case, crew conversation doesn't reflect that they dismissed the Cessna as a factor until a very short time before the actual collision. In other words, they were likely looking. The weather was good, they were given the location of the traffic, it was in a position easily visible from the cockpit, and yet they still overran the slower airplane.

It seldom happens, but it's something to think about and guard against. It reemphasizes the fact that being under radar control, as both airplanes were, is no guarantee. If told to follow another airplane and sight of it is lost, that should require immediate action to insure separation. And, climbing and descending, especially in busy areas, are critical times.

BATTLEGROUND

Much has been written about the final approach at uncontrolled airports being the great midair collision battleground. This *is* an area of identifiable hazard, but there is no way to say that solving the problem on final would eliminate a substantial part of the total problem. Accidents in which both aircraft are on final at an uncontrolled airport are numerous, but they also tend to be less serious—only a relatively small percentage were fatal in the two-year period.

These final approach collisions at uncontrolled airports tend to occur at low altitudes; 80 percent happen below 400 feet. Also, a very high percentage involve one aircraft overtaking another, and the closure rates tend to be gradual. These two factors minimize the severity of collisions on final approach at uncontrolled airports. They also teach us when to watch out for what and offer the encouraging thought that there's usually plenty of time to find, see, and avoid the other aircraft.

MORE SERIOUS

Of concern is the midair collision in which at least one airplane is moving along in a phase of flight not related to takeoff or landing. There are actually more midairs like this

than there are final approach collisions, and almost 70 percent of this type of accident results in fatal injuries to the
occupants of at least one airplane.

These generally occur at altitudes higher than the traffic
pattern, and the collision angles and closure rates cover the
spectrum. About 20 percent involve one airplane overtaking another directly from behind, but no other angle accounts for a substantial number of collisions.

The conditions of these lethal midairs follow no strict
pattern, but there are some similarities. They tend to occur
at relatively low cruising altitudes, with almost 90 percent
occurring below 5,000 feet. In most cases, both airplanes
were in normal cruising flight. In some instances, the collisions involved two training flights. Training areas are des-
ignated for flight schools, and airplanes tend to congregate
in these areas so this might be expected. There is also some
involvement between training flights and airplanes cruising
through a training area. The areas are not identified to
transient pilots, and airplanes maneuvering on training
flights are following a less predictable path than an airplane
flying cross-country. This makes both sighting and tracking
more difficult. Also, in the training airplane there must be a
tendency for both instructor and student to spend less time
looking for other traffic and more time concentrating on
the teaching/learning process.

In examining the individual reports, it is plain that many
of the midair collisions in which one airplane is not in the
traffic pattern are nevertheless closely associated with operations around an airport; that is, at least one of the aircraft
was on a local flight. The record is clear in showing that the
airspace near an airport is where the risk is highest, but

there is enough risk elsewhere to dictate constant vigilance for other traffic.

CONTROL TOWERS

The midair collisions that do occur in airport traffic areas —that airspace below 3,000 feet within five miles of a controlled airport—tend to be unusually serious. Twelve percent of the midairs in one two-year period studied occurred under the jurisdiction of tower control, and 85 percent of these were fatal. During the period, there were actually more *fatal* midair collisions under tower control than on final approach at uncontrolled airports. And, as noted, there isn't a significant difference in the fatal collision rate at controlled airports and uncontrolled airports.

NO MEASURE

While the midair collision risks can be defined and minimized just as we can do with risks in other areas, the midair avoidance task is made difficult by the fact that there is usually nothing tangible on which to hang the good decisions. As the work of minimizing weather risks is approached, we have large and obvious clouds to view. If continuing VFR into marginal conditions, the outlook changes from clarity to murkiness. If risk management is being applied to the stall/spin, the feel of the controls, what we see, and the airspeed indicator all start suggesting a problem long before the critical moment. But in midair collisions, the first inkling a pilot has of a problem is often a life-size view of another airplane framed by the windshield or a side window. Or it might just be the loud noise that accompanies a vigorous entanglement of airframes. The helicopter record suggests that development of a looking plan could bear a lot of fruit. The choppers have good visibility plus collisions. They prove that the deficiency is more in visual inactivity than in visual limitations.

SELF-MOTIVATION

The call is for a methodical visual collision avoidance plan based on the facts as we know them, on the visual limitations of the airplane, and on the capabilities of the eye.

Methodical in this must mean continuous. It is frightfully easy to fly along for hours on end with the gaze fixed straight ahead. If the windshield and windows of the aircraft are dirty, the eye can even tend to focus on the grime rather than the outdoors, making aircraft spotting that much more difficult. Sparkling clean windows can do a lot more for you than improve the view of the scenery; they can also make it easier, and probably more enjoyable, to keep up an active scan for other airplanes. If you wear glasses, do keep them clean. Do the same for your windows.

The plan should contain a requirement to look carefully all around the airplane. The point of focus shouldn't move continuously; rather, it is best to look, move a bit, look again, and continue around, and up, and down, with a pause every thirty degrees or so. Peripheral vision should pick up the airplanes that are not directly in the line of view. Once a comfortable scan has been developed, use it with diligence. Don't neglect the area behind the airplane, either. The closure rate of an overtaking airplane will be slower, but it will still be adequate if he gets his nose in your tail.

KEEP LOOKING

It is more difficult to maintain interest in scanning for other traffic while en route. We seldom see other airplanes, and it is difficult to remain motivated without an occasional reward. That reasoning wouldn't diminish the severity of an en route collision, though. The most hazardous times are when flying below 5,000 feet, when passing near airports, and when operating on airways or VFR flyways, especially in congested areas. However, some hazard exists anytime more than one airplane is flying, and colliding with the only other airplane within fifty miles is just as undesirable as colliding with one of 1,000 within fifty miles.

The hazard in relation to airline jet aircraft should not be minimized. Be especially wary when within thirty miles of an airport served by air carriers. Air traffic control procedures generally promote keeping the jets above 10,000 feet until they are within thirty miles of their destination airport, and then down they come into the airspace most often used by general aviation. The lower we fly when within thirty miles of busy airline airports, the better. It helps to listen to the automatic terminal information service, too. The jets will tend to be lower farther from the airport in the direction from which approaches are being conducted—on the southwest side in the case of approaches to the northeast, for example. It almost goes without saying that the areas of the ILS final approach course should be avoided for a distance of at least ten miles from the airport.

AT THE AIRPORT

In closer to the airport, the clear call at controlled airports is to forget that control might have some collision avoidance value when flying in VFR conditions. Base risk management entirely on seeing and avoiding other aircraft on an individual and independent basis. The prime area of hazard around controlled airports is in the airport traffic area but outside the traffic pattern.

Always check crossing runways for possible conflicts before takeoff or landing, even at controlled airports. And, for that matter, when cleared for takeoff make certain there's not one on short final. It's sensible to take these precautions. Collision avoidance is the pilot's responsibility when the pilot can see, and the pilot isn't doing his or her part unless the eye is always used to verify that what the controller cleared you to do is indeed a good idea.

At uncontrolled airports, make use of Unicom to announce position in the traffic pattern and to monitor the position reports of other aircraft, but still let the eyeball and the scan for other traffic reign supreme. Look for airplanes flying in the normal traffic patterns, nonstandard patterns, and straight-in approaches. Scan the unlikeliest spots for possible helicopter operations. On around closer to the runway, remember the characteristics of the classic final approach collision: One aircraft overtakes another below 400 feet and closure rates are low. Make sure that the final approach course is yours and yours alone.

There's no doubt that electronic collision avoidance devices will be developed, but the human eye will remain the best collision avoidance device in visual conditions. If airplanes are out there, the eye can find them if used properly. And there are airplanes there to be found. Soon after we were married, I appointed my bride as chief airplane spotter. To enhance interest, I offered to pay her one dollar for each airplane she spotted first. In a few weeks, I owed her a couple of hundred bucks. It was a good lesson for me. The old scan for traffic needed some burnishing.

8 | Mechanical Malaise

First, to identify the risk to life, Figure 6 shows fatal engine failure accidents broken down by the cause of the engine failure. This represents a recent one-year period (not the same year used in some of the other figures) and clearly shows that twins have a very high proportionate involvement in fatal accidents after engine failure. This fact always appears regardless of the time period used. For example, the IFR chart (Figure 2 on page 34) is based on the three years prior to the year used in Figure 6, and it tells the same story. In other words, it is no fluke. When studying the charts too, remember that twins account for only 15 percent of the general aviation fleet, and they have a lot more than 15 percent of the engine-failure related accidents.

The issue is confused a bit by having more failures in the "undetermined" category than any other. "Undetermined"

160

Figure 6. Engine-failure related fatal accidents. (No practice forced landings or engine-out multiengine practice accidents included.) NTSB's finding of the cause of engine failure. One year.

Fuel starvation		Actual mechanical failure of the engine		Fuel exhaustion		Undetermined		Water in fuel		Induction or carburetor ice		Improper operation		Wrong fuel		Propeller failure	
TWIN	SNGL	TWIN	SNGL	TWIN	SNGL	TWIN	SNGL	TWIN	SNGL	TWIN	SNGL	TWIN	SNGL	TWIN	SNGL	TWIN	SNGL
BE55	AA1A	BE90	BE35	BE95	C150	BE18	BE35	CVAR	C150	A560	C150	None	C182	A500	None	None	PA28
BE95	AA1B	BE90	C206	PA30	C170	BE60	BL7G	T601	C150		C182						
C310	BE35	BGLE	C210		C177	C310	BL14		C210		LUS8						
C310	C140	C310	C210		C177	C337	C172		PAJ3		PA38						
DC3X	C210	C336	HBLT		HBLT	C402	C177		PA12								
T600	GLKS	C337	HBLT		HBLT	C402	C182										
T601	PA18	PA31	LUS8		MO20	PA23	C206										
	PA22	PA31	MAU4		MO20	PA28	HBLT										
	PA28	T601	PA28		NAVN	R681	HBLT										
	PA28				PA18		MO20										
	PA32				PA22		PA28										
					PA28		PA28										
					PA28		RYAN										

means that the accident investigators could not determine what made the engine fail. In some instances, this inability to find out might be due to absolute destruction of the powerplant. Or it could be a matter of not recovering the engine, as when an airplane winds up in deep water. In most cases, however, the engine was recovered and they simply could not find a reason why it stopped running. Unidentified carburetor ice or a blockage of fuel flow that wasn't apparent after the accident could have caused the failure, but it couldn't be established with any certainty. In any event, either the engine was not recovered or there was no broken part to relate to the failure. In the latter case, these accidents were not caused by any mechanical failure within the engine.

Fuel starvation, the number two cause, comes when there is fuel in the airplane but the fuel selector is on an empty tank.

Looking at actual failures of the engine, twins were involved in *half the engine-failure related fatal accidents during this year*. To me, this is astounding. An NTSB study covering an earlier five-year period revealed that singles had a substantially better engine-failure related safety record than twins, but that study didn't show singles as dramatically better, as in more recent sample years. We'll discuss the NTSB study later on in this chapter.

It is significant that the airplanes representing the greatest numbers in the fleet—the Cessna 150, 152, 172, and 182—do not often appear in fatal accidents after engine failure. This suggests good things about both the reliability of these airplanes, and their ability to be safely landed in a hastily selected location after an engine failure. The Bonanza and PA-28, also in the fleet in substantial numbers, give an excellent account as well.

The relationship between airplane size and involvement in fatal engine failure accidents is significant. Almost half the airplanes on the list for this year are heavy singles or light twins. True, these airplanes are more likely to be up flying when the consequences of an engine failure are most serious—at night and in instrument meteorological conditions—but this is still precisely the opposite of what the public perception of risk would be. Most laymen would see the highest engine-failure related risk in the lightest airplane rather than in a heavier one.

STRIKE ONE

Even with such a convincing statistical case that the single offers no particular engine failure risk when compared with a multiengine airplane, many in big government (and big business) will steadfastly maintain that twins are safer than singles. The FAA won't even operate a single-engine airplane in its fleet and use in IFR air taxi operations is severely restricted by FAA regulations. Edicts against using singles for company transportation abound. Simply put, the unjustified prejudice against single engine airplanes is very deeply ingrained in the heads of those embracing the "more is better" theory. I've always wondered if this might not be ego-connected. To admit that a single might fill a need as safely as a twin could result in someone's big bird being taken away.

All this might change as the price of fuel skyrockets and as availability becomes difficult at times. Couple the single's excellent engine-failure related safety record with its efficiency and the airplane becomes ever more attractive.

THE PUBLIC

We'd be deluding ourselves to think that the best statistical case in the world could immediately change public opinion on single-engine airplanes and their vulnerability to engine failure. There's a basic fear that an airplane will fall if deprived of power. People ask: "What do you do if the engine stops?" Newspapers and TV combine with the uninformed in aviation to take a very active role in nurturing this fear.

Almost invariably, the paper or tube will have something like: "The engine spluttered and the single-engine plane crashed" or "witnesses reported that the motor of the single-engine plane was racing right before it hit." The fact that this happened as a thunderstorm was raging hardly seems to matter. "Engine" is the key word; "single" adds emphasis. The public perception is of brave and clean-living aviators plunging power-off to the ground, despite a valiant effort to get the engine going. The only counter is patient explanation and hope for understanding of the facts as they exist.

THEY DO FAIL!

We do have to acknowledge that engines do fail. The accidents represented in Figure 6, all fatal, are only the tip of the iceberg. In government reports of the most frequent accident types, "engine failure" usually leads the list. A lot of the accidents are not serious, but there could be far fewer total and less serious accidents if pilots would shape up and do a better job of tending to the things that keep the powerplant running. Engines seldom quit without provocation, and the problem usually originates in the left front seat of the airplane. We worry about connecting rods and valves, but pilot error causes more than half the engine failures, both total and fatal. Fuel system mismanagement (leading to fuel starvation) and fuel exhaustion are prime causes of aerial silence. This is really pilot failure, but it's considered engine failure in the accident record.

I sat flying along in my Skyhawk and thinking about this one day. I had started out from West Palm Beach, with Tallahassee listed as a destination. Tallahassee, though, was less than halfway to Little Rock, my final destination. The true plan was to go on past there to get as far as possible and ensure a one-stop flight to Little Rock. Dothan, Alabama, would be halfway. How about that? No, greedy, Montgomery would be more than halfway, so keep right on going.

The fuel gauges were down in the bad part of the range before Montgomery was reached, but the one hour's fuel reserve that I consider inviolate was still in the tanks—barely. The way I rationalized this as I flew along was illustration aplenty of how one must divorce thinking from what would be nice, what would be handy, and what would be most expeditious when contemplating the amount of fuel in the tanks. A two-stop flight would have been far more desirable than a one-stop with anxiety about fuel.

OUT OF FUEL

How large is the fuel exhaustion problem in relation to the total engine-failure picture? In some airplanes it is huge. For example, according to a five-year NTSB study covering all engine failures, almost half the Cessna 172 engine-failure accidents in a five-year period were related to fuel exhaustion. On the other side of the coin, only about 12 percent of the Bonanza engine-failure accidents were caused by fuel exhaustion. That is logical because pilots flying Cessna 172's are probably more likely to become lost and waste fuel than are Bonanza pilots—if for no other reason than the more sophisticated electronics usually found in Bonanzas. A headwind accounts for a larger percentage of a 172's cruising speed and is probably a factor in fuel exhaustion accidents. Also, more Cessna 172's are in the rental airplane fleet, where pilots might not be as current as the average Bonanza pilot. And while I have no figures to back it up, a correlation could probably be drawn between a pilot's flying time in the very airplane involved and fuel exhaustion. Once you've flown an airplane for a while, you'd be less likely to use all the fuel. You know how the gauges work and you know the fuel consumption, so there might be less temptation to kid yourself. (This could be debated. Familiarity breeds contempt in some cases.)

There's yet another side to the coin, and it can also be illustrated with a 172/Bonanza comparison. Almost half the Bonanza's engine-failure accidents are related to mismanagement of fuel or trying to run the engine on a dry tank when there is still fuel in another tank. The 172, with its simpler fuel system that can be left on "both" all the time, hardly figures in fuel system mismanagement accidents. This is an item of design, as will be covered in the next chapter, but it does help outline this part of the engine-failure problem. If you are flying an airplane with a simple fuel system, your engine failure is more likely to come from running out of gas. If you are flying an airplane with a fuel system requiring management, your engine failure is more likely to come from your mismanagement of the system. In either case, a smattering of pilot diligence will cure the problem.

THE NUMBERS

In proportionate total, singles had twice as many engine-failure accidents as twins in the NTSB study. But four times as many twin accidents were fatal, thus the conclusion that your chances of being wiped out in a twin are twice as high as in a single. And the study actually favors twins in the sense that most twins considered were "current" airplanes, usually valuable enough for loving care and valuable enough for the insurance company to require that they be flown by pilots with some experience. The light twin didn't really come into being in quantity until the mid- to late fifties, and virtually all the twins on the list were relatively young in terms of years. The singles covered a lot more ground. Homebuilts account for some engine failures, and these are all singles. Agricultural airplanes (including Stearmans) are singles, and the great fleet of airplanes built before and immediately following World War II is both old and single-engine. As an illustration of what age does to the engine-failure accident rate, it should be noted that the Cessna 140's engine-failure rate is more than twice as high as the newer 150's rate. The Cessna 170's rate is almost twice as high as the 172's rate. And some airplanes, like the old Bellancas and Navions plus the Swifts, Luscombes, and Stinsons, have comparatively astronomical engine-failure accident rates.

That the NTSB's conclusions about singles v. twins is more valid than ever is dramatically illustrated by Figure 6, covering a later period.

A SINGLE EXAMPLE

To get a picture of the risk involved, it is appropriate to take a couple of airplanes and dissect their engine-failure accident rate. The Cessna 172 is a good example of a single because it is widely used and it tends to cover the spectrum of general aviation operations. The 172's in the fleet range from business-use vehicles maintained in the finest shops, to FBO training and air-taxi aircraft, to recreational machines maintained both in good shops and under shade trees. The

172 is flown by a great variety of pilots, from student to airline transport. And despite the proclivity of pilots to use up all the fuel in 172's, the airplane has the lowest engine-failure accident rate in the single-engine fleet, as well as a lower rate than many twins.

According to numbers derived from NTSB figures, the 172 had one engine-failure accident for every 43,000 hours of operation in the five-year study period. (That does not mean there was an engine failure every 43,000 hours. It only means that for each 43,000 hours of operation, one 172 was bent badly enough after a failure for it to be considered an accident.)

Okay, now eliminate all the human error. Subtract the fuel exhaustion, starvation, and contamination; take away improper operation of the powerplant controls, including things like failure to use carburetor heat or to lock the primer. Then don't count the engine-failure accidents in which poor maintenance was established as the cause of the problem. Get down to the 172 accidents following a true failure of the engine—things breaking or failing in a properly maintained engine. On this basis, the 172 was involved in one engine-failure accident for every 303,448 hours flown.

THE REAL RISK

Go a step further now to determine the true risk to life. The NTSB study notes that 5.4 percent of the engine-failure accidents in single-engine airplanes are fatal. So, considering only the accidents precipitated by an honest breakage of the engine, an unavoidable failure while the pilot was doing and had done everything correctly, we arrive at one engine-failure-related fatal accident for every 5,619,411 hours of Cessna 172 operation. That is one every 641.5 years if you choose to fly twenty-four hours a day. Anyone who can take that number and suggest that there is something inherently dangerous about the fact that this airplane has only one engine is beyond help. Cut it in half or divide it by ten, and there's still no suggestion of extraordinary engine-related risk when flying one of the airplanes.

Admittedly, the 172 had the best single-engine record during the period studied. The PA-28 (Cherokee) was not far behind, though. And besides increasing with age, the engine-failure accident rates also trend upward with stalling speed. Retractables tend to have a higher rate, too. The latter might come from the tendency of pilots to land retractables with the gear up in any forced landing, guaranteeing enough damage to qualify as an accident even though the landing is quite successful. But as you can see in Figure 6, retractables have a rather high involvement in fatal forced landings.

A TWIN EXAMPLE

For comparative purposes, the NTSB study only includes all the details on one twin that might be considered representative. This airplane does not have the best twin record, so there are apples and oranges in our comparison, but it is still worthy of consideration. The airplane is the Piper PA-23, which designation encompasses both the Apache and the Aztec. The PA-23 fleet probably averages more age and wear than the 172 fleet. Also, PA-23's are used for a wide variety of purposes and are flown by all different kinds of pilots. The airplane starts with a raw engine-failure accident rate of one for every 32,362 flying hours, as derived from NTSB figures. Eliminate all but the true mechanical failures of an engine, and the PA-23 has a failure accident every 123,263 hours. In multiengine airplanes, 22.9 percent of the engine-failure accidents are fatal, so if the PA-23's engine-failure fatal accident were to be equal to the average for the twin fleet, the airplane would appear to have a fatal accident related to the true failure of an engine every 538,264 flying hours. This is highly theoretical because, as we will see in examining stall/spin accidents by type in Chapter 10, the PA-23 has a lower-than-average involvement in stall/spin accidents. So it would probably have a lower-than-average involvement in serious accidents following an engine failure because the stall/spin is usually the reason for an engine-failure accident reaching the serious stage.

TEN TO ONE?

There are a lot of apples and oranges plus some theoretical considerations in that comparison, which shows a sample single-engine airplane coming out ten times as well as a sample twin. It perhaps proves nothing, but the numbers are from an NTSB study and I think it reasonable to go beyond the raw figures and compare engine failures as they affect pilots who live the clean life, obtain the best available

maintenance for their airplanes, and don't run out of gas—
to say nothing of mismanaging the fuel, letting ice accumulate in the carburetor, or doing any of the other things that
pilots do to induce silence in the cabin. We can all, hopefully, convince ourselves that an honest appraisal of risks
begins (but does not end) with a look at things over which
we have no control, such as a valve or a rod breaking.

JAWS

A good twin-engine pilot listened attentively to that disser-
tation on the records of a representative single v. a representative twin and then made an offer. He suggested that
we go out off the shore about twenty miles, he in a twin, me
in a single. Then we would each secure one engine and see
what happened. He grinned like a presidential candidate,
said "Jaws," and left the discussion at that. And he had a
point. However, the purpose of the comparison was to show
the exposure to risk that is found in the single as it is used,
and I think that 5.5-million-hour figure for the 172 is encouraging.

OTHER FIGURES

To buttress the concept of the single's good record, and to
expand the sample beyond Figure 6, another year's worth
of accidents were studied individually. The only ones con-

sidered were those involving engine failure with a probable cause not related to the pilot in command. The engine quit of its own accord while the pilot was operating it properly. (This sample would include engine failures caused by poor maintenance.) One reason I did this was because a person openly mentioned the Bonanza and said something like, "What about the Bonanzas that were lost last year because of engine failures?" The fact is that there was not one Bonanza involved in a fatal engine-failure accident that year that didn't list the pilot in command as the probable cause. There was only one in the year covered by Figure 6, so this is a small part of the risk there. And, as a matter of fact, no production single-engine airplane is involved in more than one or two such fatal accidents in a given year. It is a random thing, spread very thinly and evenly throughout the fleet.

HOMEBUILTS

It is very worthy of note, too, that in this year a lot of the single-engine airplanes involved in fatal engine-failure accidents where the failure was not pilot-induced were homebuilt aircraft, many of which were powered by automotive or other nonaviation-type engines. Remember that in any NTSB statistical analysis, these airplanes are considered along with the store-bought airplanes.

AGRICULTURAL AIRPLANES

During this year, there were no agricultural airplanes involved in fatal engine-failure accidents in which the pilot in
command was not the cause. To find the dusters and spray-
ers, you have to go over to the nonfatal column. There are
a lot there, with 20 percent of the total singles ag aircraft.
This teaches a lesson that we might as well learn here as
elsewhere. The agricultural airplanes participate freely in
engine-failure accidents, but nobody is badly hurt. Why?
Because the airplanes are designed with survivability in
mind, and the pilots are wise enough to take advantage of
the safety equipment. They have and use shoulder harnesses, and most wear crash helmets. If you are ever flying
and tempted not to use a shoulder harness, remember the
wise ag pilots; they know what is good for them.

Far on the other side of the ledger is the homebuilt: A
high percentage of the engine-failure accidents in this type
of airplane are fatal. They would tend to have fewer occupant protection features, so that is logical as well as illustra-
tive.

QUESTION

All this leads to a conclusion and a question. As airplanes
are involved in fatal accidents following mechanical failures of an engine, the single comes out better. In the NTSB

study covering a five-year period, the total single-engine fleet proved to be twice as good as the total twin-engine fleet when fatal accidents following engine failure for any reason are considered. In the year covered by Figure 6, the single did even better. You can take the statistics and records apart, and everything makes the single look even better as things like homebuilts and agricultural aircraft are considered. The question is why. People often buy twins because they feel that they are "safer," yet the opposite seems to be the case.

When searching for answers, it is obvious that twins have a lot of things in common with singles. About 50 percent of the fatal engine-failure accidents happen within a mile of an airport, twin or single. Approximately the same percentage of the serious engine-failure accidents are during dual instruction, twin or single. And the engine-failure accident in the initial climb phase of flight accounts for 28 percent of the airplanes destroyed in both categories, twins and singles.

These areas of similarity are noteworthy because they show that while there might be a striking theoretical difference between singles and twins, John Q. Pilot finds the bite remarkably alike when things are done incorrectly.

With half the fatal accidents close to the airport and 28 percent of the aircraft wiped out after a failure during initial climb, we can speculate that the pilot of a twin is incapable of cashing in on any advantage that his airplane has over a single. The return-and-land after a failure apparently presents an equally difficult task to the pilot of either class airplane. Further, a failure anywhere in the pattern or a landing back on the runway with an engine out, whether it be *the* engine in a single or *one* engine in a twin, appears to present a problem of the same magnitude to the pilot, twin or single.

INSTRUCTIONAL FLYING

The roughly equal percentage of singles and twins involved in engine-failure-related fatal accidents while engaged in instructional flying shows that any asymmetrical thrust problems in twins during low-speed training operations did not unduly affect the record during the one-year period covered by my study. Training accidents are not included in Figure 6 if the failure was induced by the instructor.

REASONS

But when contemplating each class of airplane, the apparent differences in concept make it obvious that while they might have the same problems after the engine fails, they must have the problems for different reasons. And there must be reasons for more serious consequences in twins.

Simplicity is one basic thing in favor of a single. The 172 probably has the best single-engine record because there is little to malfunction and because the powerplants used in that airplane since its introduction are legendary for their reliability. (As 80-octane fuel disappears, this reliability might suffer, as there are numerous problems related to using 100-octane fuel in these engines.) Low landing speed is another advantage. If a single is flown into anything other than a brick wall or the dead center of a tree, and if the arrival is at a gentle angle and a speed not far above stall, chances are the people will fare tolerably well. Shoulder harnesses make this even better, as proven by the agricultural airplanes. The harnesses are very effective in the low-speed, low-angle accidents that can characterize even the most tedious forced landings, provided reasonable pilot technique prevails.

Apparently against the single is the fact that it does indeed have but one engine. If that one fails, there is no alternative to a landing in the very near future. However, it is possible to be optimistic and consider this an advantage, rather than a disadvantage, for at least some pilots. In the single the inevitability of the forced landing might help the pilot's mental processes. There is no doubt about what is going to happen, so do your best. In the twin there can appear to be more alternatives. To protect one's image, a twin should always be landed on an airport, right? It is probably difficult for some pilots to accept any failure of this concept, whether its elusiveness becomes obvious in initial climb or as the airplane goes low on an approach slope. The twin pilot is faced with more temptations and challenges to judgment after an engine failure, and the demand is for a top-notch professional job of planning and flying for the length of time it takes to reach an airport and land.

STALL/SPIN

In either class of airplane, the failing grade on an engine-out landing often comes when the pilot stalls the airplane. The stall/spin is the leading killer in both. And the stall/spin is where the single gains its advantage over the twin. According to NTSB numbers, 24.6 percent of the twin accidents following engine failure were of the type, usually stall/spin, that produce fatal or serious injuries. By contrast, 7.5 percent of the single-engine accidents were of this serious nature.

DOUBLE TROUBLE

The reason the twin has a relatively higher involvement in stall/spin accidents has to be related to both the nature of the machine and to human nature. The desire is to keep on flying even though half the power is gone. All the light twins have limited performance with an engine out. If the pilot fails to recognize a situation in which the airplane is not capable of climbing over obstacles, for example, and tries to make it climb over them anyway, a stall/spin is the likely result. The configuration of all the airplanes (except the Cessna Skymaster) has a lot to do with the question, too. When the engines are on the wings and when the power is halved, the remaining half is all on one side. The thrust is not symmetrical, and if the pilot lets the airspeed decay, this can cause directional control to start deteriorating. When this begins to become obvious, the pilot who is unwilling to lower the nose of the aircraft and reduce thrust as necessary to restore directional control is only seconds away from trouble. And it isn't easy to lower the nose and reduce power on the operative engine when the trees are tickling your feet.

Finally, the twin's stalling speed is likely higher than that of a single, so any off-airport landing is at a higher speed. As far as survivability goes, the prime things that count are the speed at impact and the distance it takes to stop. I've seen a single-engine airplane go through the window of an automobile showroom without great damage to the pilot. I've seen one go through the roof of a building, and I've seen them left in the tops of trees without great damage to the occupants. Twins are bigger, heavier, and harder to deposit in such impromptu surroundings without mussing your hair. And when you use all the fuel in a twin or mismanage the fuel system, the airplane is likely to require a completely impromptu arrival. Twin pilots don't make fuel mistakes nearly as often as single pilots, but it does happen.

THEORY

In theory the twin should have less involvement in engine-failure-related accidents, and the theory holds water in non-fatal accidents. But it is just not realized when serious accidents are considered. Some engine-out related accidents illustrate this.

During a dual training flight the instructor-pilot was obviously giving the student some minimum control speed drill when the airplane stalled and entered a spin. There was not adequate altitude for recovery.

A pilot flying a twin that was loaded to well over gross weight had an engine failure in initial climb. The prop on the offending engine was not feathered, but the airplane probably wouldn't have climbed anyway because of its overweight condition. There are many times when a twin should be flown well below gross weight to maintain single-engine climb capability in high density altitude conditions.

For another, the pilot positioned one engine's fuel selector to a dry tank. That engine failed, and the pilot subsequently let the airspeed decay. The final result was a stall/spin.

A scenario that constantly recurs finds a pilot losing control of a twin on an engine-out approach. In these cases, the engine usually fails en route, giving the pilot plenty of time to plan the approach. But for some reason, a proper approach slope is not maintained. The problem is usually related to premature extension of the landing gear and flaps, going low on the approach slope, and letting the airspeed decay in the attempt to correct. Once those things have been blended into the situation, most twins are incapable of making it to the runway. And the pilot loses control of the airplane in the process of trying to make it do the impossible. It is a simple matter of poor flying technique. The ending is similar to that found when a pilot of a single-engine airplane might stall and spin trying to reach a field beyond the gliding capability of the airplane during a forced landing.

GOOD OPERATING PRACTICES

The similarity of the problems encountered by single and twin pilots after an engine failure suggests that simple good operating practices to minimize the risks of engine failure might also be similar.

The time from lift-off to, say, 1,000 feet above the ground might be considered a time of maximum vulnerability to engine failure in any airplane. Once at 1,000 feet, there is enough energy stored, primarily in the form of altitude, to enjoy some options if the engine of a single fails or a few more options if one engine on a twin fails. The clear call is for a full-power climb at the airplane's best rate-of-climb speed to 1,000 feet above the surface on *every* take-off. That maximizes performance and minimizes vulnerability.

Using full power for initial climb is very important. Figures at the FAA Aeronautical Center indicate that 80.7 percent of the actual mechanical failures of engines occurred during a power change. That is a good enough reason not to reduce power in the early stages of an initial climb. If the engine spins up properly at the start of the take-off run, just leave the little darling spinning until some altitude is in the bank, in a single or a twin. Most general aviation engines are approved for continuous full-power operation, and those that have limitations are approved for full power long enough to reach 1,000 feet under most any conditions. In situations where more than 1,000 feet appears to be advantageous before contemplating the risks involved in a power loss, just keep on climbing wide open at the best rate-of-climb speed until at a higher altitude. There's simply no more efficient way to get the most altitude in the least time.

A twin pilot should be current and proficient in the transition from the twin-engine best rate-of-climb speed at full power to the single-engine best rate-of-climb speed after an engine failure. This transition must be made without allowing the airspeed to decay below the best single-engine climb speed.

ARRIVALS

On the other end of the line, vulnerability to serious accident during an engine-out arrival can be minimized by knowing how to put the airplane on a selected spot after an engine failure. In a single this becomes the power-off spot landing, ending in a touchdown at the selected location at minimum speed. In a twin it's a single-engine approach to a runway down a slope that requires about 40 percent power on the operating engine with the gear and approach flaps down. On that basis, there is some power to reduce if the approach is trending on the high side and more power to add if it is trending toward the low side. If it gets dangerously low, the gear could be retracted to cut drag. Twin or single, the simple fact that the point on the ground toward which the airplane is going remains constant in the windshield is a key to judging and managing the approach.

TO SUM UP

The twin v. single involvement in total engine-failure accidents is logical. The single does have twice as many total engine-failure-related accidents because the possibility of landing in a random area is quite high after the engine fails on a single, and some damage is likely to result from such a landing even if it offers no real hazard to the occupants of the airplane. The twin's *fatal* accident rate following engine failure is twice as high as the single's because the consequences of a mistake in a twin prove to be numerically four times worse than in a single.

The total of the single v. twin question is positive, too. The single's excellent record is a direct result of mechanical reliability, simplicity, and low stalling speed. The twin's record could be even better than the single, and would be if the human element were not so strongly against the virtues of the multiengine airplane. The pilots flying twins must only recognize the requirement for an extremely high level of proficiency combined with a complete understanding of the airplane's capability to take most of the engine-failure risk out of the twin picture.

IN ADDITION

There's another area where mechanical failure is a question and the twin has a good answer. There are a few accidents in which the failure of a vacuum or electrical system in a single-engine airplane becomes the straw that breaks the pilot's back. These systems are redundant in almost all twins, and the consequences of failure of half the vacuum or electric power are very minor. All the single-engine pilot can do is equip with warning systems to give timely word of a failure and learn to operate the airplane properly with one of the systems inoperative.

The only time an electrical or vacuum failure should be a real problem is when it occurs during IFR flight. Even here it is not a common problem. Bringing the mechanical problem column forward from IFR to generate Figure 7, we see that singles outnumber twins here, but not by a lot. And nine fatal accidents in three years doesn't identify this as a serious safety problem in singles, especially when it's considered that in every case the pilot could probably have worked around the problem—given a burst of brilliance at the proper time. All singles save one were retractables. Perhaps the more complex the airplane the more serious the failure.

	BE35
	BE35
	C210
	C210
A680	MO22
C337	PA24
C411	PA24
PA23	PA28
PA31	R112
TWIN	SNGL

Figure 7. IFR flight, fatal weather accidents. Three years. Mechanical failures including radio and accessories but not engines.

There should be one qualifier to the number of aircraft listed. Some loss-of-control accidents in IFR flying are probably related to instrument, system, or autopilot failures that are not identified in the accident investigation process. When poking around in the wreckage, especially of an airplane that hit the ground out of control at high speed, it's quite difficult to make a positive determination that absolutely nothing in the airplane failed *before* the accident. Even accepting some reasonable percentage of those accidents into the mechanical column doesn't identify this as a big factor in IFR accidents.

Two singles (the Bonanza and Centurion) offered standby electrical systems as this was being written, and more singles were sure to follow with some systems redundancy. This is all to the good.

PROPELLER PROBLEMS

There are not a lot of other mechanical things that break and cause serious problems. Propellers do occasionally fail, with disastrous results in a few instances. If a whole blade goes, the imbalance can cause the engine to leave the airplane, but this is rare indeed. Or a blade can do damage to some part of the airframe. Props are like anything else, though, and respond favorably to tender loving care and unfavorably to neglect. Good maintenance is the key to avoiding propeller problems.

BIG SINGLE

One other check mark must be put on the twin's side of the
ledger before leaving the subject of the relationship between mechanical reliability, the number of engines, and
accidents. From a practical standpoint many twin-engine
airplanes have two engines because they need two engines.
An airplane of their total horsepower, speed, and capacity
simply would not be practical with one engine. The redundancy of systems is deemed necessary, and the weight
of the aircraft and the wing loading are just not such that
you would want to accept the absolute risk of a random
landing if the only engine should quit. Once an airplane
reaches a certain size, there is no question that two engines
might be required. Below that size, the argument will rage
on for years. And if twin pilots will get their act straight,
they might someday make the record more logical than it is
today.

9 | Miscellaneous Hazards

Most all of the serious accidents fall in one of the categories covered, but there are a few hazardous items left over. These do not account for a substantial number of annual problems, but that doesn't soften their hostile nature.

WITH A BUSTED SOMETHING

The NTSB's computer calls one troublemaker "attempted operation with known deficiencies in equipment." That would cover a multitude of mechanical sins uncovered during preflight or maintenance and not repaired before flight. Or it might relate to a failure of something remedied by an airworthiness directive that had been overlooked by the pilot or shop servicing the aircraft.

Airframes are sturdy and trustworthy items, and it's rare indeed to find an accident that is related to some honest failure of the bird. When something *does* break, it is usually after the pilot overloads the structure during maneuvers or after a loss of control.

Poor maintenance causes a few problems, but serious accidents caused by the pilot blasting off with a known deficiency outnumber those caused by an honest failure of airframe parts 2:1. And in many of the honest failure cases, operation with a known deficiency could have been a companion cause. If a pilot goes off with a known loose widget and that widget fails, the cause would fall in both categories.

PROPELLERS

There are a number of accidents involving people v. propellers. As noted in Chapter 3, many of these occur at night. In most cases, the person hit by the propeller is not a pilot. Some bystanders and ground personnel walk into props, but most participants seem to be passengers.

A passenger might disembark to go do something for the pilot, such as turn on hangar lights or make arrangements for aircraft parking, and walk into the propeller. Perhaps the passenger is just entering or leaving the aircraft when the engine is running and goes in the wrong direction. I think all pilots have had passengers say, "Oh, don't shut it down; I'll just hop out." That is bad news. The only safe way is not to allow anyone to enter or leave the airplane with the engine running. On a twin some feel it is okay to let people enter and leave with the engine on the door side secured and the other one running, as the airlines often do, but remember that the airlines have ground personnel watching the passengers to make sure nobody gets over on the wrong side of the airplane.

STARTING

Some people v. propeller accidents are related to hand propping. Propping is a lost art, and it seems unwise to let anyone who is not experienced attempt a hand start.

There is a related accident where the scenario calls for the pilot to prop the airplane without anyone at the controls and for the airplane to go do its own thing, wreaking havoc on the way. In one such accident, the pilot left a nonpilot inside, the engine started, and the airplane took off with its passenger and flew around for some time before crashing.

It is clearly unwise to prop an airplane without a pilot seated at the controls. There might be one exception: We used to prop J-3 Cubs from behind with one hand near the throttle and one hand on the prop, and I can't recall anyone having trouble with that procedure. But I do remember one lad, an accomplished J-3 pilot, trying to do the same trick on a Champion one morning and letting a perfectly good airplane impale itself in the side of the hangar.

CONTROLLER'S ERRORS

There are a few fatal accidents every year in which an air traffic controller was deemed to have made an error. Controllers are human, and while they generally do their job with more uniformity than pilots, it's important to keep tabs on them and watch for a mistake. It is healthy to keep track of position when being vectored, especially when there is high terrain around or when there are obstructions near an airport. Someone telling you which way to point the airplane and the altitude at which you are expected to fly isn't a signal for the pilot to become a thoughtless robot.

The responsibility for the safe conduct of a flight belongs entirely to the pilot in command. It is a mistake to feel that any responsibility can be transferred to the ground or that controllers can affect a recovery from a precarious situation created by the pilot. People on the ground can aid a pilot by furnishing information; the pilot must interpret the information, apply it to the flight, and make the decisions.

VORTEX TURBULENCE

Vortex turbulence from heavy aircraft can be very upsetting to smaller aircraft, and a few years ago it appeared that this might become a major safety problem. Airports with a high concentration of both air carrier jets and light airplanes were ripe for wake turbulence accidents, and a number of them occurred. The FAA did good work, though, with research into the nature of wake turbulence, with educational programs, and with air traffic control procedures designed to preclude wake turbulence encounters. In one recent year, there was only one serious wake turbulence accident, and it had a bit of freakish nature. The pilot departed behind a jet airliner, and everything would have been okay had the pilot not aborted the takeoff because of a rough engine. If the climb had continued, the flight path would have been above the jet's wake; on the abort, the pilot descended into the wake turbulence and lost control of the aircraft.

The principles of wake turbulence are relatively simple. The wing tip vortices settle, so always maintaining a flight path above the path flown by a preceding heavier airplane will keep the vortex safely below. If flight must be conducted below a heavy aircraft, the rule is to fly at least 1,000 feet below. The vortices tend to start degenerating some by the time they have settled 1,000 feet. Whenever in doubt, add some extra time or altitude.

SIMPLE MISTAKE

There is one basic, recurring error that is always perplexing: Every year a few pilots attempt a takeoff with the control locks installed. The results are quite predictable. This even happens in airplanes with internal control locks—devices that are in the full view of the pilot before the takeoff is attempted. A person would have to ignore completely the "controls free" part of a checklist to fall victim to control locks.

MORE MINOR ITEMS

In moving away from serious accidents, it is best not to dismiss things that don't hurt as meaningless. Every fender bender counts. It has been said that even after a minor accident, a pilot must fly for 500 hours without incident lest he be classified as "accident-prone." Circumstances would have to be considered in any such classification, but there is no doubt that all accident types should be studied and avoided. The most minor accident can be a sign of weakness in technique or judgment and an indication of bigger and worse things to come. There's also a quality of "total awareness" that enables safe pilots to land on their feet every time. A minor accident reflects a flaw in this awareness.

As might be expected, a high percentage of the relatively minor mishaps are landing accidents. These often happen in high wind conditions, as covered in Chapter 4, but there's one more thing to offer on this subject.

The Ercoupe, general aviation's first tricycle-gear airplane built in quantity, had its share of landing accidents as it moved into the fleet in force right after World War II. The Ercoupe's problems were precisely the same ones that lead to many landing accidents today, and the Ercoupe sales organization outlined it quite well in a 1948 newsletter, from which the following excerpts are made:

no difficulties with landing should be encountered if a
few simple and easy rules are taught and observed. . . .
The most prevalent error in landing the Ercoupe is *too
much airspeed on final approach*. . . . It further appears
that some pilots are under the impression that the Ercoupe nose gear should be used like a battering ram. . . .
The Ercoupe should be landed in a nose-up attitude. . . . Excellent results can be obtained from a full-
stall landing. . . . Don't land nosewheel first; it won't
work for long. . . . Don't shove the wheel forward.

Sympathy for the Ercoupe salesman's dilemma is easy to
find. As tricycles became the standard, other airplane
builders watched as pilots developed the same bad habits
that plagued the Ercoupe thirty years ago. Despite the tricycle gear, 30 percent of the total accidents occur during
the level-off, touchdown, or rollout phase of flight.

A NTSB study offers another illustration of how the tricycle is no cure-all. It shows four tricycles at the top of the
list for involvement in hard landing accidents; current production taildraggers are far down the list. Perhaps the tricycle makes it look easier than it is while the taildragger is
obvious in its challenge.

SPEEDY

The first thing mentioned in the Ercoupe newsletter, excessive airspeed on final, is still a primary cause of landing
accidents. Pilots *know* that the stall/spin is a leading acci-

dent type, and flying with a little extra airspeed margin above the stall can seem prudent even when there's no wind-induced turbulence to harass the pilot. Too much of a good thing turns to bad, though, and excessive airspeed can only lead to bad landings regardless of wind.

Landing characteristics are tailored to an approach speed 30 percent above the stall. There is certainly enough margin in this. Approach a bit slower, and the airplane is still manageable through the flare and to touchdown. Carry a bit of extra speed because of turbulence and wind gusts, and the landing can still be graceful. Go too far either side of that normal approach speed, though, and the situation will deteriorate. Too slow, and you wind up in the stall/spin chapter; too fast, and there might be a relatively minor accident or things could progress into a major event if a go-around is attempted late or if the airplane goes into rough stuff off the end of the runway at high speed.

THE MESSAGE

The tricycle expects to be landed on the rear wheels first and to have the little nosewheel lowered to the runway rather gently. Most landing accidents occur when pilots do it backward and land on the nosewheel first.

We purists have long tried to sell the full-stall landing as a solution to the problem, but it is as hard to sell in tricycles today as it was thirty years ago, when the Ercoupe was exploring the world of the general aviation pilot v. the nosewheel. Many pilots are just not going to work at a full-stall landing unless they absolutely have to. And there is a viable alternative, called the *attitude landing* by some. If those who reject the full-stall landing would only at least accept the attitude landing theory, the majority of the landing accidents would cease. Either way works.

All you must do is pick an attitude for touchdown that results in the main wheels touching first. The airplane isn't allowed to touch until it is in that attitude, which insures that the nosewheel isn't involved in the initial ground contact.

The annual cost of landing accidents is high, and it's too bad. The tricycle landing gear offers a lot of advantages, but the rules of landing really remain much the same as in the old taildraggers.

OH, I FORGOT

In some of those landing accidents, the pilot's approach and touchdown technique might be perfect, but an error of omission might cause the whole thing to end as an embarrassing disaster. Forgetting to extend the gear on a retractable or retracting it after landing is rather common. There's an old saying about this: "There are pilots who have done it, and there are pilots who are going to do it." It's not that bad, but everyone flying a retractable should be alert to the possibility. I use the mental prelanding GUMP drill (gas, undercarriage, mixture, and prop) on every arrival, whether or not the airplane is a retractable. After landing, I also find it best not to retract the flaps, fiddle with the cowl flaps, or attend to anything other than directional control and stopping until clear of the runway. Gear and flap switches are in different positions in different airplanes, and not moving anything until there is time to study the situation should help avoid retracting the gear instead of the flaps in the landing roll. Most airplanes do have switches to preclude gear retractions when on the ground, but these switches often don't function when there's not a lot of weight on the wheels, as is the case early in the landing roll.

The circumstances surrounding gear-up landings are often unusual, with the pilot distracted from the normal routine. One standard gear-up theme is a landing following a go-around. The gear and flaps are extended for the first approach, and on the go-around the gear is retracted and the flaps brought to a climb setting. The go-around pattern is flown at a rather low altitude. Flaps are extended on base or final for the second try, and quite a lot of power is used to fly the airplane to the runway. The first bad news the pilot gets is when the throttle is chopped to land. The gear horn blows at about the same time the tender belly starts scraping the runway and the prop blades begin flailing the surface.

Once the mistake is made, and the airplane has contacted the runway, it can be very dangerous to try to salvage the situation. There have been instances where a pilot has heard the prop tips hitting the runway and has managed to pull up, extend the gear, and land safely. But there have also been instances of the pilot attempting a go-around after the prop has suffered too much damage, resulting in an accident much more serious than a simple belly slide.

There are other variations on the theme, but that covers most of them. Just remember that even the most minor accident is serious in the sense that it might reflect a basic weakness that will lead to more serious things in the future.

10 | Problems Peculiar to Make and Model

Airplane salesmen often make the mistake of using safety as a sales tool. One ploy is to point out some allegedly fatal flaw in a competitor's airplane in an attempt to scare the customer away from it. Another is to use an accident as an example: "You remember old Joe? Rest his soul. If he had been flying one of *my* airplanes, he'd have made it."

Some seem to have a vendetta against certain airplanes, too, and in sensational exposés attempt to make the machine appear as a flying coffin.

In either case, competing salesmen or someone trying to sell papers, such tactics are not constructive. Generally, the only way to make a case against any specific airplane is to lift it out of context and concentrate on its weaknesses while ignoring its strengths and the weaknesses of similar airplanes. In truth, statistics can be used to crucify or praise

198

any airplane. And given similar uses and equal exposures, the accident rates of all contemporary airplanes are fairly close. When there are substantial differences, there are usually logical reasons. The nature of use and the user have a considerable influence on the airplane's accident record.

This doesn't mean that design has no effect on safety. It most certainly does, but not in a clandestine manner. Airplanes just don't keep secrets—at least not for long. For example, the Cessna 150 has a simple on-off fuel system, whereas the Piper Cherokee has a left-right system that requires management. The 150 has virtually no involvement in fuel system mismanagement accidents; the Cherokees have relatively frequent involvement in that type accident. Piper's newer trainer, the Tomahawk, also has left-right selection. The Beech Skipper has an on-off system. To show that disagreement about the best system continues after the engineers are finished, proponents of the Tomahawk insist that its left-right fuel system is better because it can be used to teach fuel management. The Skipper's system cannot.

The individual pilot's cue is to learn enough about each airplane flown to avoid the things that cause trouble. Perhaps an argument could be made to take the features from every airplane that prove to minimize participation in particular accident types, such as simple fuel systems, and standardize them for all airplanes. But that would stifle design creativity and would lead to a standardized airplane that might not have much utility. We must be allowed to assume that the pilot has some sense, and can adapt to differences in airplanes that enhance particular designs.

NTSB STUDY

Figure 8 shows the fatal accident rates (per 100,000 hours) of some contemporary airplanes. These numbers were taken from a couple of NTSB studies and are offered as somewhat ancient history. While the studies were released in 1979 and 1980, they covered the 1972 through 1976 period. Too, accident rates per 100,000 hours are always suspect because nobody really knows how many hours are flown. Still, this figure is useful in considering relative accident rates.

The Bellanca sticks out like a sore thumb. We'll go into that in detail further on.

When the Bonanzas, the 33, 35, and 36 are compared with the Travel Airs and the Barons, the 95, 55, and 58, the single-engine airplanes appear to fly with a lower fatal accident rate than the twins.

The Cessna 150 and 172 do beautifully when compared with other brands as well as when compared with their siblings. This, perhaps more than anything else, can be used to illustrate the misconception that exists about aviation safety. If you parked a fleet of Cessnas on the ramp and asked a panel of "experts"—FAA people, airline and corporate pilots, flight instructors, and TV and newspaper people (the latter representing the public)—to pick the airplane that would be safest on a ten-hour trip, based on the record, how many do you think would pick the 150? How many would pick the 172 as second? No, most would

Fatal Accidents per 100,000 Hours

Beech 33, 35 & 36 Bonanzas — 2.55
Beech 95, 55, 58 Twins — 2.83
Bellanca 4-place retract — 5.68
Cessna 150 — 1.34
Cessna 172 Skyhawk — 1.47
Cessna 182 Skylane — 2.02
Cessna 210 — 3.09
Cessna 310 — 2.18
Cessna 337 Skymaster — 3.06
Cessna 421 — 1.63
Mooney M-20 series — 2.44
Piper PA-23 series — 2.60
Piper PA-28 series — 1.97
Piper PA-31 Navajo — 1.13
Piper PA-32 series — 2.74

Figure 8. Fatal accident rate per 100,000 hours flown, by make and model; NTSB data for 1972–1976. From special studies released in 1979 and 1980.

go to the 421, 337 or the 310. The 150 looks like a flivver, the others have two engines. That makes them safer in the eyes of some. (Per mile, the 310 and 421 would compare more favorably because they are about twice as fast.)

In the Pipers, the studies show that the single-engine PA-28's do well in relation to the twins. The PA-31 (Navajo) comes out very well.

Use these NTSB numbers from the 1972–1976 period to compare similar airplanes from different manufacturers. Figure 9 lumps the heavy singles together. The Beech, Cessna, and Piper airplanes are close together, the Bellanca sticks out. The twins, which are more likely flown by non-professional pilots, appear fairly even in Figure 10.

BELLANCA

Why does the Bellanca appear to have such a bad record? For one thing, the designation covers virtually all four-place Bellanca retractables—from those made right after World War II up through the Vikings. And, as will be shown later, the older an airplane gets, the worse its fatal accident rate per 100,000 hours becomes. But, pause: The Bonanza does much better and that designation also covers airplanes built over a period of more than thirty-three years. So that's not a good excuse.

To give the Bellanca another chance, I examined the record for the 1976 through 1978 period, the latest three years available at this writing. The rate developed is the percentage of the registered fleet that was involved in a

Fatal Accidents per 100,000 Hours

Figure 9. Heavy singles. Fatal accident rate per 100,000 hours. NTSB 1972–1976 data.

Figure 10. Owner-flown type twins. Fatal accident rate per 100,000 hours. NTSB 1972–1976 data.

fatal accident in a three-year period. (Developing a rate based on the percentage of the fleet involved in accidents is certainly as accurate as an hourly rate where the airplanes are of similar speed and nature and are likely to be used in the same manner.)

The 1976–1978 record for the heavy singles is pretty even. (The Beech airplanes were considered separately there.)

Beech 33	.0061
Beech 36	.0093
Beech 35	.0112
Bellanca	.0146
Cessna 210	.0128
Piper PA-32	.0191

The Bellanca doesn't stand out there, and in evaluating risks for tomorrow's flight, the more recent history should be of greater value. Also, this seeming change in the record from one period to the next shows how one must be calm about rates and records and seek further information if one particular airplane stands out.

CESSNA 414

The Cessna 414 (a pressurized cabin-class twin) had an accident history a few years back that illustrated two things. Developing accident rates on airplanes that are not in the fleet in large numbers is likely to be an inaccurate business. And, an airplane can appear to have a horrible accident record, at least for a year or so, through no fault of its own.

The 414 is very similar to the Cessna 421; the 421 outnumbers the 414 by a substantial margin; and yet in one year there were *seven* 414's in fatal accidents compared with one 421. The 421 record was about what you'd expect; the 414's was hard to believe. Its fatal accident rate for the year was something like 4½ times as high as the general aviation fleet, and ten times as high as the rate in business and corporate flying where the 414 is most often used. I first thought there must be a mistake, but a careful check indeed reveals seven 414 accidents in that year.

UNRELATED

The careful check also showed that not one of the accidents was directly related to the airplane.

One 414 pilot descended into a mountain; improper IFR operation was given as the reason.

A 414 was destroyed when its pilot went below the minimum descent altitude on a night, nonprecision approach.

A pilot without an instrument rating was caught at 19,000 feet on top of an overcast in a 414. The overcast was entered on descent, control of the airplane was lost, and the results were obvious.

Another pilot without an instrument rating continued VFR into IFR conditions in a 414, with disastrous results.

A pilot who had been denied a medical certificate flew a 414 into a mountain on a dark night.

A 414 pilot returning from a trip tried some aerobatics in the traffic pattern. A stall followed a low-level roll.

And a private pilot stole a 414 and apparently crashed at sea.

There is only one airplane-connected item to consider. The 414 is a basic pressurized twin. It often sells to people stepping up to that class airplane. Two of the accidents involved VFR pilots in IFR weather. It is very safe to say that any combination of a pilot without an instrument rating (and instrument proficiency) and an airplane like the 414 is likely to be lethal. It is simply not practical to extract transportation from any airplane without IFR capability; the faster and higher the airplane flies, the more impractical and unsafe it becomes.

PERSONALITY

Just as an airplane like the 414 might have a bad time with VFR pilots when they start flying high and far, other airplanes have their particular problems with pilots. They aren't always what you would expect. For example, an NTSB chart on overshoot accidents shows the Cessna 172, which has big flaps, with a higher overshoot accident rate than the Ercoupe, which has no flaps and can't be slipped because of no (or very ineffective) rudder control. Perhaps the Ercoupe is so plainly demanding of accurate glide path control that pilots try harder. On the other hand, Cessna 172 pilots might feel those big flaps can be used to patch up the worst of approaches.

On hard landings, the taildragger Cessna 180 has an

accident rate less than half that of the 182—again opposite of what you might expect. The 180 is very plain in its demand. It rears back on its big main gear and issues a clear warning: Stay away unless you know what you are doing. The 182, on the other hand, sits level and with a gentle, friendly look seems to say, "Come fly me, I'm easy." But the combination of a downspring in the elevator control system, and an almost level stalling attitude in the ground cushion with full flaps and forward center of gravity, leads to a relatively high involvement in nosewheel damage accidents.

The full panel, radar, de-icing, avionics and autopilot of a 414 won't patch up a pilot's botch job any more than will the flaps of a 172 or the tricycle gear of a 182. The pilot has to use the equipment properly. They can fiddle with and tweak airplanes forever and not make one that will completely compensate for a dull pilot.

SERIOUS MATTERS

That specific airplanes are vulnerable to certain areas was obvious in Figures 1 through 7.

The fleet of airplanes flown VFR into fatal weather-related accidents (Figure 1 on page 21) is what you would expect. The Cessna 150 doesn't appear very often because it is primarily a training airplane. There's plenty of cross-country flying in training, but it is under the supervision of an instructor. Instructors are generally very conservative about the weather for student solo cross-country (and dual cross-country as well) so the 150's aren't often out in marginal VFR conditions.

What do Cessna pilots fly after receiving the private license? They fly 172's and 182's, and there are a lot of those in the VFR weather accident column. This doesn't mean that the 172 and 182 are any less safe than the 150 when it comes to VFR cross-country flying. It is, instead, a reflection on the judgment of pilots at the particular time in their flying career that they use 172's and 182's for traveling.

The same thing is probably true with the Pipers. There are a lot of PA-28's on the list. In this case, the airplane is both trainer and follow-on airplane, depending on which model PA-28 is involved. If separated, the high likelihood is that the emphasis would be on the more advanced PA-28's in the VFR weather accident columns.

There are some twins and high performance retractables in the VFR weather accidents; these must often be charged to a pilot using an airplane in an unsuitable manner. As speed increases, the real definition of "marginal" VFR must be altered upward. If three miles is minimum visibility in a Cessna 150, then six miles should be minimum visibility in a 310. Time counts more than distance in visibility (unless the 310 pilot can really think twice as fast as the 150 pilot), and this has led many a pilot into a hillside.

Considering the loss of control in VFR conditions, there does not appear to be any conclusive relationship between this type accident and specific airplanes in Figure 1. In fact, if you take a spirited airplane like the Bonanza, one that doesn't give third chances and will get to you quickly if control is lost, and the 172, which will give chance after chance to a relative klutz, the rate of involvement in loss-of-control accidents in a year might be closer than you think. (Airframe failure accidents were also considered as loss-of-control.) On Bonanza 35's, .00073 of the fleet was so involved: the number for the 172 was .00046. For further comparison, the Cessna 182 was .00037 and the Piper PA-32 was .00144. The Cessna 210 was not involved in a loss-of-control VFR accident in this year. That suggests that the airplane is stable laterally (which any 210 pilot will vouch for), and that use of one-year periods should be restricted to discussions like this. The sample is not large enough for the development of conclusive accident rates. There has been controversy over the Bonanza in airframe failure accidents (which almost always involve loss of control) and that will be treated fully and separately.

IFR

There were more twins than singles in IFR accidents in the three years covered by Figure 2 on page 34. That's logical. As mentioned earlier, twins probably don't fly any more IFR hours than singles—they might even fly less—but they probably fly more night IFR. That's a more difficult task and leads to a higher accident rate. We also saw that twins had a very high incidence of IFR engine-failure fatal accidents when compared with singles.

Does any particular type airplane stand out in IFR accidents? To me, it would have to be the Cessna 337. This airplane isn't in the fleet in large numbers, yet it is involved in several different IFR accident types. This is a clear example of how an airplane's accident record might be determined more by who buys it than by the airplane itself.

The 337 (Skymaster) is a centerline thrust twin. The specter of an asymmetric-thrust-induced loss of control is eliminated. And some pilots probably buy a 337 because they feel it's a safer twin to fly with a lower level of proficiency when compared with a 310, for example. But that lower level of proficiency must get them on the final approach course on a dark and bumpy night. The 337 is only easier after an engine failure; even there, its record isn't nearly as good as it should be.

COMPLEXITY OF THE MATTER

It might be tempting to dismiss the predominance of twins and retractables in IFR accidents with the thought that simple singles don't fly much IFR. That's not true, though. Even on the grungiest days, you hear Cherokees and Skyhawks making their way through the weather and the IFR system. Certainly they don't fly IFR in proportion to fleet size, but there are still a lot of them out there.

In fact, when there's no ice or thunder around, the light singles probably have the greatest IFR safety potential of any general aviation airplanes. Their slower speed means the pilot doesn't have to think as fast. A few degrees off heading results in a slower movement of the nav needle away from center. In the unlikely event of an engine problem, their gliding and touchdown speeds are lower. If there's an instrument problem, they are easier to fly on partial panel—or at least the consequences of a mistake are probably less serious. They put less total demand on the pilot and can be flown at the same speed and in the same configuration in cruise and on approach. The gear is down, and there's no need to fool with the flaps. With weather avoidance gear—radar or a Stormscope—they would be as good as anything in relation to thunderstorms (as long as the pilot concentrated on avoidance), but there's no way to help a light single on ice. The rates of climb are just too low.

I think the light single pilots do a good job of staying out of the IFR accident column because the airplanes leave more time for the fine points of instrument flying. The only trouble is that light singles are far from being as suitable for long-distance travel as the retractables and twins. This makes plain the task for IFR pilots. You can fly a 210 or a 337 as safely as a 172, but you have to work harder. And if problems start developing, you might have to work a lot harder to keep the risk down to what it might be in the 172.

IN THE DARK

Figure 3 on pages 60–61, which covered night fatal accidents is also more a reflection of what type pilot flies each airplane than the airplanes. VFR night cross-country in marginal weather is *the* most lethal type of flying. What kind of airplanes are flown on VFR night cross-country? The ones in the stack in Figure 3—most of them four-place relatively simple singles. Weather is such an overwhelming part of the night VFR accident problem that it's tempting to dismiss the rest without a mention, but there are a couple of interesting items.

Alcohol and night: Lots of Cessna 150's there, as many in fact as in all the rest of the night accidents combined, including VFR in adverse weather. (If 152's are included, alcohol is one short of being equal to all the rest.)

Why is the 150 the prime aircraft for alcohol-related night missions? It must fall victim to the relatively new pilot who wanders to the airport after imbibing, and takes his friendly trainer for a little ride. Doesn't work. And even the most ardent proponent of the foolproof airplane would be hard-pressed to imagine a way to make an airplane "safe" for a drunk pilot.

STALLING AND SPINNING

You find a quite different set of airplanes in the fatal stall/spin accident table, Figure 4 on page 107. Gone are a lot of the traveling airplanes. Here are the trainers and recreational airplanes. It's the first table with homebuilts, Taylorcrafts, J-3's, a Porterfield, a Stearman, and a lot of two-place Bellancas (Citabrias and kin). There are the airplanes used for knocking around, which would include buzzing. The Cessna 150 outnumbers the 172 by a lot, because the 150 is more likely used for play and the 172 for travel.

The entire stall/spin problem can't be attributed to

knocking around and playing. The problem is bigger than that. A lot of airplanes are lost in initial climb. These appear to be a cross-section of the general aviation fleet. If anything, the list might be slightly more representative of the airplanes you'd find based at a relatively small airport, where initial climb performance is likely critical.

Stall/spin problems after engine failure are more common to homebuilt airplanes than are some other things, but there are no particular exceptions there.

The go-around is a small part of the total, with no great surprise. There are more 150's there than anything else, which might be expected. The 150 has big flaps; a go-around requires good technique, and the 150 is most often flown by student pilots.

The high-wing v. low-wing involvement in midair collisions was pretty well covered. It's obvious from Figure 5 on page 143 that midairs are more likely to involve training airplanes (150's and PA-28's) than any other.

The relationship of engine failures to airplanes offers no pattern not previously discussed.

AIRFRAME FAILURE

The question of airframe failure in flight is very directly related to configuration as well as make and model. Quite a lot of controversy was generated in 1980 by allegations that the Beech model 35 Bonanza is a "death trap" because of airframe failures but, simply put, an objective look at the record fails to show that the Beech 35 is alone in any proclivity toward airframe failures in flight. The subject is much broader than a particular airplane, and one can only examine the motives of anyone who so limits the subject.

To begin, consider the recent airframe failure rate for some contemporary airplanes. Figure 11 is based on 1976 through 1978, the most recent NTSB records available as this was compiled. The rate given is the percentage of the fleet of each airplane that was involved in an airframe failure during this period. The airplane with a zero rate is included for reference. Airplanes not included either had one or no failures in the period, or were in the fleet in such small numbers that one accident could cause a huge variation in their rate.

It is plain that the V-Tail Bonanza 35 only stands out when compared with its straight-tail siblings, the 33 and 36. In fact, when compared with heavy singles from other manufacturers, it falls fairly well within the average. Do be aware that the annual number of airframe failures is relatively small for all airplanes, and these rates can move around with time. For example, Figure 12 is based on the NTSB's study of single-engine airplane airframe failures in flight in the 1972 through 1976 period and shows a somewhat different picture. It is, I think, significant that the PA-32 is low in the 1972–1976 study and higher in the 1976–1978 study. In the latter period, more of the PA-32's were retractable Lances, and retractables have always had a higher incidence of airframe failures in flight. The NTSB study lumped the Beech 33, 35, and 36 together; the failures were virtually all in 35's as is reflected in the previous chart that I generated. Also, for some unknown reason the NTSB combined the Cessna 205 and 210. The 205 isn't a

Percentage of the Fleet Involved—1976–1978

Beech 35 V-Tail Bonanza .0023
Beech 33 & 36 .00
Bellanca 4-place retract .0021
Cessna 210 .0020
Piper PA-24 .0012
Piper PA-32 .0025

Figure 11. *1976–1978 airframe failure rate for heavy singles, in percentage of the fleet involved.*

Airframe failures per 100,000 hours—1972–1976

Beech 33, 35, & 36 Bonanzas 0.58
Bellanca 4-place retract 1.49
Cessna 205/210 0.34
Piper PA-24 0.42
Piper PA-32 0.24

Figure 12. *1972–1976 airframe failure rate for heavy singles. Rate per 100,000 hours. NTSB data.*

retractable, thus its rate would likely be lower and the 210's airframe failure rate somewhat higher than indicated in Figure 12. (The rate in Figure 12, based on NTSB data, is per 100,000 flying hours; the rate in Figure 11 is the percentage of the fleet so involved in a three-year period. The relationship of the airplanes to each other within each chart is the point of consideration.)

STRAIGHT-TAIL BONANZAS

The question that begs for an answer is why the Beech 33 and 36 (the straight-tail Bonanzas) have such a low involvement in airframe failures in flight, a type accident relatively common to other airplanes of similar weight and configuration. The question is enhanced by the fact that all Bonanzas—straight and V-tail—have light ailerons and neutral roll stability, things that are considered as contributors to a loss of lateral control, which usually precedes a loss of longitudinal control. And once control of both is lost, the result is usually an uncontrolled collision with the ground or an airframe failure in flight.

There are no pat answers, but there are some reasonable explanations.

One model of the straight-tail Bonanza was approved as an aerobatic airplane and, indeed, the horizontal tail of these airplanes bear more than a passing similarity to that of the Navy's T-34 trainer. The 33 and 36 must have much of the strength that was developed for this airplane. On the other hand, the V-tail 35 has no forebear that gave it structural strength over and above any other airplane. The 35 has undergone some structural changes over the years, primarily to allow higher gross weights, but a desire to make the airplane a bit overstrength was probably in the back of someone's mind as the structure was changed. Old 35's shed wings when they were overstressed, so the wings were made stronger. The tail of newer ones often fails first. If they strengthened the tail, the failure might move back to the wings, although this hasn't happened with the 33 and 36.

The Bonanza is very clean aerodynamically and it has very responsive controls. If control is lost, speed builds very rapidly; the failure speed of a 35 airframe has been estimated at over 400 miles per hour. If failure at that speed could be designed out of the airplane, something else would come up. In fact, on one 35 dive test the windshield blew out before anything else failed.

The matter seems rather clear. If you want a Bonanza with an airframe failure rate about on a par with airplanes from other manufacturers, the 35 is fine. If you want one that's hell for stout when compared with the fleet in general, go for a 33 or 36.

The Mooney M-20 is another very strong airplane. Its abnormal strength came when the airplane was converted from a wooden tail and wing to a metal tail and wing. The story goes that when converting to metal some years ago, Mooney didn't want to have to do a lot of structural substantiation for the FAA so they made a metal version of the old wood parts. It was thus *very* strong. Also contributing would be the Mooney's high elevator forces and the single-axis autopilot that was standard on the airplane for a number of years. The high elevator forces help guard against pilot-induced overloads. The single-axis autopilot runs full-time and keeps the wings level or returns them to level when the pilot releases the controls.

THE DEVIL HIMSELF

There's another factor to consider in the airframe failure record. As in other areas, it relates to who operates the airplane and how it is used. There is no way to reduce this factor to numbers, but it must be considered in any objective analysis of an airplane's accident history.

Everyone has heard the tales about there being nothing more lethal than a doctor in a Bonanza. If you'll watch, too, most doctors who fly Bonanzas fly V-tail model 35's. It is about the classiest looking airplane in the fleet, it stands out on any ramp, and it attracts pilots with one of two personality traits: a big ego, or a love for classic machines. How many V-tail Bonanza pilots do you know who drive Dodges and Plymouths? They more likely drive to the airport in a car that has the classic lines and crisp performance of their airplane. And they are likely successful in business or in a profession. When they try to become equally successful in getting their Bonanza to the destination regardless of weather, trouble pops up—especially if the pilot isn't instrument-rated. The average V-tail pilot simply isn't the type to take no for an answer. Fliers of the straight-tail 33 and 36 are likely to be more practical folks. For one thing, the V-tail has a rather severe aft-loading limitation that isn't shared with the other airplanes, and any truly practical pilot would opt for a 33 or 36—just as a practical driver might walk by a flashy sports car and buy a VW bus.

There's no question in my mind that personality plays a strong role in V-tail Bonanza weather accidents. Given equal structural strength, this in itself might make it logical for the Bonanza to have more trouble than others in this area.

Some of my best friends are V-tail Bonanza pilots (two of them also own a Pitts, to illustrate the point), and I hope they (and other Bonanza pilots) don't take offense at this bit of amateur psychology. But I do hope they recognize the potential problem.

HOW IT HAPPENS

Every airframe failure accident doesn't involve a Bonanza, but almost every one does involve a retractable.

This should not be considered evidence that retractables are harder for a person to fly in clouds or in turbulence, or that they are weaker in any sense. The certification requirements are the same whether or not the wheels fold up into the airplane's bottom. The retractables are simply clean aerodynamically. Let them go their own way and speed buildup is likely to be rapid. The red line, the never-exceed-speed, can be quickly passed. It is for this reason that retractables are more prone to airframe failures than other single-engine airplanes.

Airframe failures are often related to a spiral dive, a

condition that comes to an airplane naturally. Most airplanes will wander off into a screaming diving turn if left alone. Put a pilot without instrument training in a cloud, and the airplane's natural tendency to enter a spiral dive is probably encouraged by the pilot. A hasty turn after entering weather might upset the pilot's orientation and cause him to disregard or misread the instruments. Certainly when a pilot inadvertently penetrates weather and decides to retreat, there would be some desire to turn as quickly as possible. This can lead to overbanking. A classic case involved a turbine-powered airliner penetrating a squall line: The pilot started to turn around, encountered turbulence, and simply let the airplane wind into a diving spiral. The red line was exceeded, and the airplane was pulled apart in a recovery attempt.

In some airplanes, a spiral can be a stable situation, an equilibrium where the forces trying to steepen the spiral are finally equalized by the aerodynamic forces trying to return the airplane to level. The angle of bank will be steep (probably around sixty degrees) and the nose-down pitch attitude might be twenty-five degrees or so. The airspeed will be much higher than the trim speed, at which the airplane had been flying in level flight. The airplane might not fail in the spiral itself because of constant pressures.

A spiral-dive related airframe failure might come as the pilot recognizes the situation and begins to do something about it. The unusual attitude recovery drill in a high-airspeed situation is to level the wings and then correct the pitch attitude. Pulling out of the dive is likely to have emphasis in the pilot's mind, too, especially if the airplane has flown out of the clouds and the ground is near, or if the altimeter is on a low value and unwinding rapidly. This is where the airplane might be broken. Or, it might even break itself.

Remember, the spiralling airplane is going faster than its trim speed. Just leveling the wings will make the airplane zoom upward of its own accord, creating great stresses while seeking the trim speed. A pilot might make the situation worse by pulling back on the wheel and putting even more stress on the airframe.

TAIL

The horizontal tail is sometimes the first thing to fail. The download on this structure can be extreme at high speed and with the elevator deflected upward in a recovery attempt. Once the horizontal tail starts to go, school is out.

Many airframe failures occur when the airplane is quite near the ground. In this situation, the pilot might recognize the inevitability of the situation and give one last and mighty tug on the wheel. Remember, any time an airplane is being flown above the maneuvering speed, it can be damaged or destroyed with the controls. The farther above the maneuvering speed, the easier it is to do.

In the case of a screaming, diving spiral, there might not be any real salvation in some airplanes. What hope there is would be found in recognizing the situation with some altitude left and in minimizing the stress in the pullout. This might be done by adding a little forward pressure to the wheel as the wings are leveled—or at least by not pulling back on the wheel. This will minimize loads the airplane will put on itself while seeking its trim speed. The only chance for success in pulling out of a high-speed dive comes in doing it very gently.

The airframe failure's relationship with the retractable makes a strong suggestion. When coming close to where this type accident might occur—the prime risks are VFR pilots in IFR weather and any pilots in or near thunderstorms—consider extending the landing gear. With the gear down, any speed buildup after a loss of control will be more gradual, and there will be more time to react and less speed to deal with in a recovery. In most cases of airframe failure, the gear is still neatly tucked into the bottom of the airplane at the time of failure, and power hasn't even been cut. (Flaps, even approach flaps, shouldn't be used to make the airplane aerodynamically less clean after a loss of control; the limit-load factor is lower on most airplanes with extended flaps, meaning that it takes less g-load to overstress the wings.)

When airframe failure occurs in thunderstorm areas, pilots are likely to think in terms of the turbulence breaking the airplane. This doesn't often happen, though. Airframe failures in and around thunderstorms tend to develop as elsewhere. First, there is a loss of lateral control, then a loss of longitudinal control and a big speed buildup. In heavier airplanes, longitudinal control might be lost first, on encounter with a big updraft that would stall the airplane. Lighter airplanes would tend to fly on through such a stall rather quickly. There's no way to know, but I'd bet that when an airplane breaks up in a thunderstorm, it usually happens after the pilot initiates a turn. When you are trying to keep the wings level, the basis of what you are trying to do is as far away from a lateral upset as possible. Roll into a thirty-degree bank, and you are perhaps halfway to a lateral upset. Giving up half the margin in the turbulence of a thunderstorm puts a great demand on the pilot. Whatever happens, it is rather rare for an airframe failure to be documented that relates only to a catastrophic encounter with turbulence.

FRYING PAN OR FIRE?

Unfortunately, airplanes that are not involved in airframe failures in flight don't tend to have a better weather accident rate than the ones that are broken up in flight. Perhaps this indicates that if you save a pilot from one thing as he moves in over his head, something else will get him.

Fixed-gear airplanes have an accident that is very similar to those in retractables caused by a pilot losing control in weather, but the fixed-gear hits the ground whole after loss of control. And in a high percentage of the airframe failure accidents, the downward progress of the machine might well have been such that it would have hit the ground rather hard whether or not it failed.

THE OLD BIRDS

The relationship of airplane age to the accident rate has often been explored and the conclusion is always that older airplanes have more accidents. Figure 13 shows how some

Fatal Accidents per 100,000 Hours

Aircraft	Rate
Cessna 120/140	1.70
Cessna 150	1.34
Cessna 170	3.15
Cessna 172	1.47
Cessna 195	3.75
Cessna 210	3.09
Navion	3.80
Piper J-3	4.73
Piper PA-22 Tri-Pacer	3.28
Piper PA-28	1.97
Stinson 108	2.28
Swift	9.27

Figure 13. Fatal accident rates per 100,000 hours of selected aircraft. NTSB data for 1972–1976. From special studies released in 1979 and 1980.

older airplanes compare with newer ones, especially of similar configuration and from the same manufacturer. In-
evitably, they don't do as well, though the old Cessna 120
and 140 is very nearly as good as the more modern 150.
This information is from the NTSB's 1972–1976 study. It
might be taken with more grains of salt than usual because
their flying time and fleet size data on older airplanes is
probably more inaccurate than for newer airplanes. Also, I
think the accident record on older airplanes will improve in
the future. The nostalgia craze is leading people to restore
those fine old birds to like-new (or better-than-new) condition, and pilots will probably fly them more carefully as
they become scarcer.

The Globe Swift has a catastrophic accident rate. This is
another example of a personality rather than an airplane
problem. I used to own a Swift so I can speak from experience.

The Swift isn't a very good airplane, nor is it a dangerous
airplane. The stall characteristics are brisk but you only
have to see it once to develop a healthy respect for the
airplane. The airplane sends a plain message: "Twist my
tail and I bite." The Swift is far sleeker looking than it is
fast, too, and the jaunty little taildragger just happens to
attract very hot pilots. It did me: Twenty, leather jacket,
and $1,500 in my pocket, I had to have one. And when an
old friend remarked that it looked like a little French
fighter, I *knew* I had made a wise choice. Fortunately I
tried to use my Swift for transportation and didn't get carried away with playfulness—where this airplane probably
plays "gotcha" better than some others. Or maybe it
doesn't. Maybe its appearance leads pilots to play harder

than with more mundane airplanes. Who, for example, would feel very playful flying an old Stinson?

The engine-failure accident is one that will probably bug the old airplanes forevermore. Many have engines that are out of production, and this means parts are harder to get and good overhauls are harder to come by.

THE LATEST AND GREATEST

Switching from the old to the brand-new, there have been and always will be problems with new airplanes. There are two forms of trouble. One is mechanical, the other is with flying technique.

Mechanical problems with new airplanes usually result in a lot of headlines and attention, but not in serious trouble for a lot of people or for a long period of time. This is because failure in a new airplane is treated with urgency. After a design has been around for awhile, something failing might be dealt with slowly. There are a lot of those airplanes out there, and if such a thing never happened before, the tendency could be to look beyond the design, to maintenance and damage history for an answer. But if a brand-new one winds up as a trail of aluminum through the woods, it's a different story.

Cessna's Conquest is a good example of this. The airplane was quickly grounded after an inflight breakup was related to a problem with the tail. A fix was developed, but the airplane was quickly grounded again after a tail problem was found in a fixed airplane. The response was fast:

Keep them all on the ground until yet another fix is found. It was tragic that one airplane had to be lost, but the simple fact is that there's no way to learn all there is to know about an airplane in a flight test. Almost everything, sure, but not *everything*. That we've had so little serious trouble over the years is a reflection of quite good work in all the engineering departments.

TWIN COMANCHE

An example of how the relationship between aircraft handling qualities and flying technique can cause problems came with the Twin Comanche. In the first few years after its introduction in 1964, the Twin Comanche developed a terrible accident record. A lot of the accidents occurred on training flights, and were of the stall/spin variety. In the standard scenario, one engine was cut; the airplane then entered a spin that flattened, so that it hit the ground in a flat spin. As the airplane aged, it became more a traveling machine than a training machine and its accident rate now compares very favorably with other twins and high performance singles.

The Twin Comanches had training trouble because of a dumb FAA procedure, and because nobody blew the whistle on this early in the proceedings. A contributing cause was the fact that the Twin Comanches replaced Apaches as multiengine trainers at a lot of schools, and the new airplane had substantially different handling qualities than the older one.

The contributing FAA procedure called for Vmc (minimum engine-out control speed) demonstrations to be done as low as possible, but not lower than 500 feet above the surface. Some FAA offices interpreted this literally, and had instructors teaching and applicants doing Vmc demonstrations at 500 feet.

Why would the FAA want pilots flirting with loss of control at such a low altitude? Their reason was logical. The posted Vmc of an airplane is based on developing full power on the operative engine. Without turbocharging, full power is available only at sea level in standard conditions. When flying a normally aspirated twin at altitude, Vmc moves below the stall. So, do the demonstration as low as possible to keep Vmc above the stall.

Trouble came to the Twin Comanche because Vmc was very close to the stall, even at low altitude. Originally, Vmc was given as seventy knots. (It was later arbitrarily raised because of the accident problem.) Stall speed is sixty-five knots, so a literal interpretation of the FAA's procedure led instructors to have students flying within five knots of the stall at altitudes as low as 500 feet. This combined with brisk stall characteristics and the obvious loss of control after an engine-out stall to create the problem. Even FAA inspectors were not immune to this type accident and for a while it seemed that the FAA was licensing the survivors of its prescribed multiengine curriculum. The amazing thing was the slowness with which they moved on this. If it had been a structural weakness, the airplane would have been grounded. But because the FAA itself was a major part of the problem, it took a long time to straighten things out.

TOMAHAWK

When Piper introduced the Tomahawk, a lot of people thought it might be like the Twin Comanche and start off with a terrible stall/spin accident record. The Tomahawk has very brisk stall characteristics, and will spin at the drop of a hat. And it is a replacement for the 140 Cherokee, an airplane that is very docile at the stall. It spelled trouble. But the Tomahawk experience in the first year or two suggests that the airplane isn't having a lot of stall/spin problems. Maybe we do learn from experience.

PILOT TIME IN TYPE

There has to be a relationship between a pilot's flying time in an airplane and the risk involved in flying that airplane, but it might not be as significant as a lot of other factors. And this can certainly be influenced by the quality of a check-out. Looking at the ultimate training process, the way the airlines check out pilots in something like a 747, we see very little relationship between time in type and serious accidents. Some of those lads flying the big airplane have virtually no time in the airplane when they start flying it on scheduled trips. But they do have a lot of time in the simulator plus enough ground school to understand the machine and its systems. And they have an excellent safety record.

There is a relationship between the type accident a pilot has in a general aviation airplane and his experience in the airplane. Hard landing accidents, for example, are likely to come early. Looking at two serious accident types, stall/spin and weather, we see that pilots with less time in the specific airplane than average have more stall/spin trouble than pilots with experience in the airplane they are flying. Time doesn't help with weather, though. Pilots with more experience in type tend to run afoul of weather more often than do pilots who are new to an airplane. Systems, especially fuel systems, can also be a problem until a pilot becomes familiar with the machine.

However it is sliced, there's no mystery to airplanes, and the record strongly suggests that a properly trained pilot can fly any airplane with an equal degree of safety—given good judgment and an understanding of the risks. An important part of "properly trained" is in learning about characteristics or systems that might demand a little extra effort of the pilot. Given this understanding, any pilot can make a liar out of anyone who suggests that one airplane is less safe than another.

11 | The Intrepid Airperson

All pilots have straight teeth and a crooked smile. All eat properly, none are fat, eyesight is crystal clear, and not one aviator misses daily exercise. The annual physical exam ensures that everything is always 100 percent.

If all that were true, either everyone would want to become a pilot because of the health benefits, or few people could qualify to be a pilot. In real life the actual physical profile of pilots covers the spectrum, with the exception of those suffering from automatically disqualifying problems such as heart trouble and diabetes that can't be controlled by diet. In fact, only about 1 percent of the people taking FAA physicals fail. That shows that an average person does quite well. There is no substantial accident history related to in-flight disability caused by health problems, too, so the criteria for medical certification must be more than adequate.

When a pilot does keel over at the controls, leaving a nonpilot to try and salvage the situation, it creates headlines. This might give the impression of a relatively frequent happening, but the record shows only a dozen or so annual cases of pilot incapacitation, and a substantial number of these are related to the monumental consumption of alcoholic beverages, which will be discussed in the next chapter.

FROM THE HEART

True instances of airborne incapacitation are usually related to the heart and usually involve pilots in their forties. Some older, some younger, but the age number starts with a four in most of the cases. Perhaps this is evidence of a stressful time in the lives of the type of people who fly. Business and personal demands tend to peak at this time. Careers are cast in stone (or turned to sand), and kids go off to expensive colleges. The businessman-pilot probably pushes harder during these years than any other, taking a toll on the old pump. Maybe people who use airplanes push hardest of all, too. Use of the airplanes is certainly evidence of a desire to maximize effectiveness.

Still, incapacitation is not a large problem. Those who are concerned about it can obtain some peace of mind, too, by having frequent passengers understand the operation of radio and autopilot equipment along with the rudiments of flying. Cases have been recorded of completely inexperi-

enced people landing complicated airplanes rather successfully, so the outcome isn't always bad even when the
passenger has had no training.

Shoulder harnesses could be very helpful in more ways
than one in case of pilot incapacitation. They can help
soften the results of any impromptu flying performance on
the part of a passenger, and if the disabled pilot has a harness on snugly, it would tend to keep him from falling into
the controls. Unfortunately, the normally more desirable
inertia-reel harnesses wouldn't serve the purpose of keeping
an ailing pilot straight in the seat because they activate only
on g-forces.

A couple of items for incapacitation: On-board oxygen
might help in reviving someone, as might spirits of am-
monia.

CARBON MONOXIDE

Carbon monoxide poisoning is an infrequent but possible
cause of pilot incapacitation that affects passengers on an
equal basis. This often comes from cabin heaters—either
the exhaust muff heaters in single-engine airplanes or com-
bustion heaters used in twins. If fumes are noticeable, if a
headache develops, or if there's a giddy feeling, suspect
carbon monoxide. The cure is to turn off the heater, open
vents or a window, use oxygen if it is available, and, in the
case of a suspected problem in a single, lean the mixture
severely. Less carbon monoxide is produced at leaner mix-
tures. Carbon monoxide detectors are available, too, and a

good preventive measure is to have the exhaust system carefully checked on a regular basis.

BASIC HEALTH

Even though it is not documented, the pilot's physical well-being probably figures in more accidents than the relatively few attributed to incapacitation or impairment for reasons other than alcohol. To contemplate these, we almost have to rely on imagination and personal experience. Anyone who has flown much has recognized a relationship between how a person feels and how a person flies, and if we recognize this relationship and work around it, minor things are less likely to cause problems.

FATIGUE

Fatigue is probably the most frequently encountered problem. Professional pilots might not have this problem because operating the airplane is their job. They should reach the airplane rested and ready to work. Most of us, though, operate the airplane as an adjunct to work or play instead of as a primary activity. For example, we get up early and fly somewhere to work or to play all day, then we fly back. The morning flight might be at top efficiency, but the evening flight comes after mind and body have put in a full day.

Frequently, accident reports say that an accident was caused by pilot error—the hapless lad flew the whole thing into a mountain at night—when you just know that a bit more than that was involved. The pilot was probably tired and wanted very badly to get home. The obvious cause of the accident might have been the pilot flying into the mountain, but the causes behind the cause were physical and mental fatigue and the desire to get somewhere. Especially when an accident occurs at night, fatigue might be considered as a possible contributing factor.

Two things that minimize the effects of fatigue when flying after a hard day's work are oxygen and food—a lot of the former and little of the latter. Oxygen has the capability of sharpening both night vision and the mind, and I've found it very beneficial to use oxygen at all altitudes when tired, especially at night. And don't go off hungry, but big meals seem best left until later, until after the flight. A person is less likely to doze off or become decidedly dull when lightly fed than when stuffed. Another effective fatigue fighter can be an unscheduled stop for a soda and a stretch. Those able to take catnaps might even get a short snooze on the airport couch during the course of a relatively short rest stop.

NOISE

Noise is a big fatigue producer and one of the easiest to manage. Earplugs can make a loud prop airplane as quiet as a jet, and they cost very little. Wearing them during a long flight makes an appreciable difference in fatigue. It also helps prevent the hearing loss that plagues pilots who have spent many hours in noisy airplanes. Do you hear me?

MEDICINE

Much has been written about medicines and flying. As might be expected, "never" is the most frequent admonishment in connection with medication and flying. Certainly antihistamines do make some people drowsy, and no prescription drug should be taken before flying unless approved by the prescribing physician or preferably by an aviation medical examiner. But some physicians dispute the outright prohibition on flying after taking certain mild medications and say that it is okay for the pilot to fly as long as he feels unaffected by the medication. That might be okay for some but risky for anyone who is prone to engage in self-deception.

OTHER FACTORS

Things affecting the thought processes probably play an even larger role than actual physical health problems. It has been noted that people experience basic ups and downs, which can be related to airplane accidents. And it has long been held that people prone to do something untoward might be more likely to do so when the atmospheric pressure is low. So there might be a correlation between the thought processes leading to an accident in bad weather and low atmospheric pressure. The two usually go with each other.

BE PRACTICAL

It wouldn't be possible to make practical use of an airplane based on flying only when one feels at the crest of the mental and physical wave and when the atmospheric pressure is high. The saving graces are being able to recognize our less than optimum days and our ability to compensate for any weaknesses that develop. A methodical approach to flying is the best way to do this. We don't want to base aeronautical success on the fast thinking and perfect co-ordination that might come on our very best days. We should instead base success on procedures and flying techniques that withstand the tests of time and temperament. Then the good days will be just that much better. The same thing holds true for atmospheric pressure. The clear days with high pressure are the easiest anyway, and that is when we probably feel sharpest. On the grungy days, we might tend to match the sky with our mood, but the flying had best be according to a methodical plan that gets the proper things accomplished at the proper time.

PANIC AND CONFUSION

The self-discipline required to perform when not at peak is
relatively easy to develop. In times of extreme stress, that
self-discipline is more difficult to find. Search, though, because the outcome of some difficult situations is likely to
hang on the pilot's ability to control himself as well as the
airplane.

An example comes to mind. A private pilot without an
instrument rating started out VFR but wound up flying in
turbulent clouds. He made contact with stations on the
ground and was doing a tolerable job of flying and maneuvering the airplane toward an airport, despite the fact
that he was in a hostile environment. The pilot remained in
control of the airplane and himself until the time of fuel
exhaustion. Then the airplane was allowed to dive into the
ground at high speed. Panic would have to be considered in
this case. After an initial serious error, the pilot had been
doing well at salvaging things until a climactic situation
developed. The chips were down. An extremely difficult
situation was at hand, and it had to be managed properly
and immediately. Then he blew it. The airplane was lost, or
given up, and nature took its course. If reason had pre-
vailed, if the flaps had been lowered, and if the airplane had
been slowed to a normal gliding speed, the impact might
have been reasonably soft and the incident might have had
a much happier ending.

THUNDERSTORMS v. THOUGHT PROCESSES

Many of the airplanes lost in thunderstorm turbulence could also be related to a pilot not managing the required thought processes for survival.

A thunderstorm is a terrifying thing. The turbulence is severe, and the rain makes unbelievable noise. The airplane is difficult to control at best, and the overall impression is one of occupying a small space between a large rock and a very hard place. Some might give up the ship and accept whatever comes next.

I recall a letter from a pilot who lost control in a thunderstorm and spent several moments just contemplating his fate before taking some action. He felt doomed, and it took him a bit to convince himself that he might still have a chance. Then he pulled the throttle back, the airplane flew out the side of the storm, and he was able to recover and fly on. Others might keep trying, but worsen the predicament by doing the incorrect thing, by trying to turn around quickly and get out. Trying a steep turn in strong turbulence is a good way to lose control of an airplane. Still others seek to solve the problem with the radio. In a trying time, most pilots do have a tendency to use the radio in an attempt to talk their way out of a situation that really responds only to the pilot's mind, eye, and hand. The time for talk is before, when asking the questions necessary to locate and avoid the storms.

The ones most likely to succeed in an area of turbulence

would be the ones who set the priorities and methodically work at them, despite the hostile environment. Certainly nobody but the pilot can fly the airplane in such a situation. The pilot who realizes that and scoots down in the seat under a tight belt and works as calmly as possible at keeping the attitude about level and the angle of bank as close to zero as possible has the best chance of emerging from the other side of a storm, battered but unscratched.

ANY TIME

Thunderstorms are just one example of an instance where a pilot's control of himself is a critical part of success. A forced landing or engine-out landing in a twin would also be a good example, as would the handling of an icing situation or any other possible but not normal situation. The decisions are critical in each case, as is the execution of the plan. The time allowed is often short, with few seconds available for procrastination.

CONFIDENCE

The role of confidence is a major one when a pilot is confronted with a difficult situation. Whether it be a thunderstorm, a forced landing, or whatever might come along, the pilot who feels confident that he can master the situation has a better chance of finishing things successfully. If over-confidence got the pilot there in the first place, that is bad, but if confidence can help the pilot think clearly and act intelligently in handling the airplane, that is good. However it works out, any pilot who is overwhelmed with the feeling of being a passenger, not in complete control of the flight, has a serious problem.

OXYGEN

Moving back to keeping the body going, oxygen is the best thing we can buy to help our well-being while aloft. It is not only a good fatigue fighter, it can also become a necessary personal item before the regulations begin requiring it above 12,500 feet. There's no way a person who lives near sea level can fly all day at 10,000 feet and remain sharp for a demanding approach and landing at the end of a flight without using supplementary oxygen. It is good to have oxygen available on all long flights, regardless of the altitude, and it should be considered necessary for all operations above 10,000 feet. It is wise to lower that altitude at night.

YOUNG AND OLD

Chronological age is considered by some to be a safety consideration and there are some things in the record to suggest a relatively minor relationship between a pilot's age and the ability to operate airplanes safely. Whereas the nonfatal accidents tend to run in proportion to the number of pilots in any given age group, the total accidents don't quite conform to the pilot population.

The youngest pilots tend to do the best. The 16-to-19 age group has fatal accidents at a rate of about one-half the percentage of this group's representation in the total number of pilots. This is quite the opposite of their experience in automobiles.

Young pilots do well for a number of reasons. They learn fast, their reflexes are quick, and most have a lot of respect for airplanes. The young pilot is probably less prone to buzz or press on into weather. This is in contrast with the young automobile driver (possibly the same person) who might speed or otherwise operate an automobile in a reckless manner. Also, a high percentage of the pilots in this age group are student pilots, and students are subjected to more direct supervision. A substantial number of the young pilots who do have accidents tend to have at least a private certificate, which suggests that their record becomes more nearly average once they are out of the nest and off on their own.

TWENTIES

The 20- to 24-year-old pilots do well, too, but the best showing of all is in the 25-to-29 pilot group. This is the largest group numerically, and it is fairly evenly divided between student, private, and commercial pilots. If a figure were available on the average annual hours flown in relation to pilot age, I would guess that 25- to 29-year-olds would probably run average or a little above average, too. A lot of the active flight instructors are about this age, and they would balance any lower activity among students, who are more numerous than in the older pilot age brackets.

Pilots in their twenties probably do well for the same reasons as the teenagers. The sharp reflexes are still there, they catch on fast, and for some reason the young seem less prone to fly on into the face of obvious adversity.

MOVING ON

Once we move into our thirties and forties, we don't do as well. The 30- to 34-year-old pilots are slightly above the line in fatal accident involvement, and the peak is reached in the 35- to 39-year-old group. I did a similar study eleven years ago and found the same thing to be true. The 35-to-39 group had the worst record then, too. At that time, I offered the thought that these pilots were the ones who might have learned to fly right after World War II while in their early twenties, on the GI bill, and that the record might be a reflection on the quality of training during that period. If so, then the 45-to-49 age group should reflect this weakness in a study conducted eleven years later. It does to some extent, but it is not as far above average now as the 35-to-39 age group. So that might be considered an accident-prone period in the life of all pilots.

Why should people in their late thirties have more problems with airplanes than pilots of other ages? Nothing stands out when studying individual accident reports. The probable causes follow the averages. The percentage of students, private pilots, and commercial pilots involved is as might be anticipated: Not many students, a lot of private pilots, and a few commercial and ATRs were at the controls in a rather large sample of 35- to 39-year-old-pilot fatal accidents.

If one thing stands out, it is the quality of the airplanes that pilots in this age group destroy. It is good equipment. If the line is drawn right above the Cessna Skyhawk class of airplane, and all airplanes above that line are classified as high-performance airplanes, then almost 70 percent of the accidents involving 35- to 39-year-old pilots were in high-performance airplanes in the sample studied. This is perhaps an age where a person has had time to succeed and to afford the good things, and a time when that same person is more inclined to manage the risks of flying rather poorly.

Some 35- to 39-year-olds spin in, some descend into the ground on IFR approaches, some continue VFR into adverse conditions—it's all there, in both singles and twins. There's just more of it.

OVER THE HILL

Pilots in their forties also have more accidents than might be expected. They too have their accidents in rather nice airplanes, and there appears a discernible tendency of this group, especially the 40- to 44-year-old pilots, to have an above average number of weather-related accidents. The most common weather problems follow the familiar script of a private pilot without an instrument rating continuing VFR into adverse weather conditions.

When a pilot reaches forty, might he or she develop more of a "damn the torpedoes" outlook about weather and press on? Might we tend to develop a more overwhelming feeling about the importance of our presence in a given place at a given time and take more risks to achieve that goal? The record suggests that reaching this age doesn't have much influence on parting the clouds for a VFR flight, nor does any business or professional success on the ground. When at the controls of an airplane, a pilot is a pilot. What he or she does on the ground just doesn't count when flying.

FIFTIES

When in their fifties, pilots do a bit better, with the best record coming in the 55-to-59 age group. A very high percentage of the accidents involving pilots in their fifties are weather-related, which would be expected. At this age, the playfulness that might lead to buzzing should be gone, and there should be a level of maturity that would preclude doing other careless or reckless things with the airplane. It's too bad this couldn't carry through to the pilot's relationship with weather, but it doesn't.

SENIOR PILOTS

The senior pilots, those over sixty, had more problems than I expected in this sample. The sample was enlarged to double-check this involvement because in the age/accident study done eleven years ago the senior-pilot involvement was just about average. Even with a much larger sample, the older pilots tended to be involved in fatal accidents more often than expected.

One thing did compromise this finding. A number of the pilots involved were exactly sixty. That would tend to reinforce the theory that age does not have a direct bearing on accidents: if those an even sixty were taken out of the sample, then the pilots sixty-one and older would have a record that is about average.

The senior pilots who have accidents do it in weather more often than not, and, as noted earlier, this age group does not figure in pilot incapacitation accidents in any abnormal number.

AS MIGHT BE EXPECTED

In total, I think we find that all the aberrations in the record that can be related to physical well-being are logical. If a pilot is aware of them, they shouldn't cause trouble. Managing fatigue and not flying when ill or when under the influence of medicine is pure common sense. Being aware of the possibility of a carbon monoxide problem is quite simple. Use of supplementary oxygen at appropriate times is a reflection of basic wisdom.

Avoiding the risks generated by the mind is much more difficult. The thread here runs throughout the accident picture. In every area the failures generally have little to do with the pilot's physical abilities or the airplane. Perhaps we can do the most effective work by always flying on the basis of a self-challenge and -response system: "Is this a reasonable thing to do and the proper way to do it?" If the answer is always an unqualified "yes," then the risks are probably being managed rather well.

12 | Alcohol and Illegal Drugs

A high percentage of the pilots in our land probably enjoy an occasional drink. And it is safe to say that a high percentage of the pilots who drink operate automobiles after having consumed moderate amounts of alcohol. But most pilots abstain before flying. The rule says eight hours from bottle to throttle. That rule is certainly not broken as often as the rules governing autos, where about half the drivers in fatal accidents are intoxicated. Why do we do better in airplanes? Because it takes little imagination to know that while there might be loving whisky and fighting whisky, laughing whisky and crying whisky, there just isn't any such thing as flying whisky. Even the mild euphoria that comes from a couple of drinks can be all but debilitating in an airplane.

Of the small number of pilots who do try to mix alcohol and flying, a certain percentage might be reasonably successful. For example, I know one fellow who often has a drink before lunch or a beer with lunch, and then flies his airplane in the afternoon. He is in violation of the regulations, but he has no trouble and can see nothing wrong with his practice. And he may never have any trouble unless he changes the script. If one leads to two and two leads to three, then he might find the hand on the throttle overwhelmed by the bottle.

THE SCOPE

The size of the drinking and flying problem might be outlined by the fact that in an average year about 6 percent of the pilots flying airplanes involved in fatal accidents are deemed by the NTSB to be impaired or incapacitated by alcohol. The FAA has always suggested a somewhat greater alcohol involvement than has the NTSB. They consider any alcohol a factor, whereas NTSB usually considers it only when the level is consistent with that used by most states for classifying automobile drivers as intoxicated. In other words, you can break the FAA's eight-hour rule without the NTSB taking note. So it is safe to say that over 6 percent of the pilots involved in fatal accidents had some alcohol in them. I doubt that the figure would be a lot higher, though.

The nature of the alcohol-related accident appears easy to outline. Over 90 percent of the accidents are fatal. There just aren't really enough nonfatal alcohol-related accidents to bother with. Also consider the fact that fatal alcohol-related accidents tend to outnumber convictions for drunk flying by about 4:1, and the picture becomes quite clear: Those who are caught are more likely to be caught by the airplane than by the law. And when the airplane collects for the pilot's transgression, it does it with total vengeance.

One part of this picture probably isn't completely accurate. I can't quite buy the fact that alcohol-related accidents are more lethal than midair collisions or stall/spin accidents and doubt if they really are. Virtually all the fatal alcohol-related accidents are identified as such because, under the circumstances, the pilot is not in a position to avoid the check for alcohol that is part of the accident investigation procedure. But after a nonfatal accident, a pilot who has had a few drinks might very easily avoid a blood-alcohol or other incriminating test. Said another way, if you knock yourself off doing it, you are sure to get caught. If you survive, the chances of being caught diminish—for that outing, at least. The rules are likely to be changed to require that a pilot submit to a test for alcohol after an accident.

SUGGESTION

The nature of the flying and drinking accidents offers a strong suggestion on who is involved in this type of accident. Circumstances usually suggest that accidents are *not* caused by social drinkers flying an airplane after a drink before lunch or a normal ration of liquor during an evening cocktail hour. And there are not a lot involving impetuous youthful aviators.

The strong suggestion is that most pilots who have accidents after drinking must be people with quite a serious case of alcoholism. The amount of alcohol consumed and the fact that a lot of accidents happen in the daytime tend to confirm this. In some cases, there is plain evidence that an incapacitating amount of alcohol was consumed by the pilot in flight. The highest level I have seen on a report would have resulted from the pilot, a 200-pound man, drinking about a fifth of 100 proof in the hour before the accident.

In about 20 percent of the alcohol-related accidents, the airplane just flies into the ground or the trees. In many such cases, the alcohol level suggests that the pilot might not have seen the ground or trees coming or didn't comprehend or care.

The alcohol level in an ATR-rated pilot who flew a twin into some trees on final, for example, was enough to cause a substantial deterioration in all processes. If you weigh 160 pounds, toss off about *nine* ounces of 100 proof in short order and you'll get the point, or forget the point, or something. Anyway, that's about how much this pilot had on board.

Some significant points made by Figure 14 outline the alcohol problem over a two-year period. Both fatal and non-fatal accidents are included, but most alcohol-related accidents that make it to the record as such are fatal.

That thirty- or forty-year-old pilots are involved in a high percentage of these accidents is apparent in the first two

Night Pilot by age/flying time	Day Pilot by age/flying time	Uncontrolled descent (includes cont'd. VFR into bad weather)	Stall/Spin	Buzzing, low-level acrobatics	Hit ground, objects	Fuel exhaustion, mismanagement
24/4						
38/4						
19/22						
20/23						
38/24						
38/59						
40/65						
29/90						
28/90	27/57					
32/103	77/89					
37/107	48/191					
43/150	19/208					
26/176	48/242					
48/180	46/284					
39/189	45/300					
29/193	44/316			AA5A		
44/200	36/399			BE35		
52/200	30/400			BL7A		
28/209	54/414			C150		
39/248	41/488			C150		
50/250	37/536			C172		
37/282	45/540			C172		
55/350	39/700			C172		
41/492	28/726			C180		
26/500	57/752	A100		C182		
31/509	31/798	BE35		C182		
36/537	60/1036	BL14		C182		
52/603	51/1500	C150		C207		
59/646	54/1500	C150		C421		
33/650	46/1800	C150		HBLT		
47/650	48/2250	C150		PAJ3		
44/1465	44/3000	C150		PAJ3		
52/2300	49/3085	C172		PAJ3		
30/2402	37/3300	C172	AA1B	PAJ3		
37/2850	35/4247	C182	BL7A	PA18	BE50	
39/3000	45/4274	C195	BL7A	PA22	C150	
27/3900	50/5017	C207	C150	PA23	C150	
31/5506	44/6507	C310	C152	PA24	C152	
29/6450	33/6890	DHC2	C185	PA24	C182	
53/6875	43/13151	PAJ3	C195	PA28	C182	AA1A
34/7000	36/UNKN	PA18	MO20	PA28	C206	BL14
55/7200	44/UNKN	PA18	PAJ3	PA28	NAVN	C150
32/UNKN	49/UNKN	PA24	PA11	PA28	PA18	C150
38/UNKN	53/UNKN	PA28	PA20	PA28	PA24	ERCO
49/UNKN	58/UNKN	PA28	PA32	PA34	PA28	PA28
53/UNKN	69/UNKN	PA28	TCFT	TCFT	PA28	R680

Figure 14. Total alcoholic-related accidents. Two years.

columns, where pilots are listed by age and flying hours. The number of accidents that occur in the daytime might be considered a surprise.

In the night column, there are a lot of low time (under 300-hour) pilots represented—far more than in the daytime column. In fact, where about half the pilots in night/alcohol accidents have less than 300 hours, only a few of the daytime folks have less than 300 hours. This strongly suggests different personality disorders for night- and day-drinking pilots. The pilot involved in a day/alcohol accident is much more likely to have a sustained and serious problem with the habitual use of alcohol. The fact that he was drinking during the day and then tried to fly an airplane is a clear sign of fouled-up priorities.

At night, many of the pilots with under 300 hours could have been as much victims of misunderstanding as of chronic alcoholism. Being relatively new to aviation, they might not relate to the tremendous difference between flying and driving, and the absolute necessity of separating alcohol in any amount from the former. Those who bite the dust at night are younger, too. The average age is six years younger than the daytime pilots.

Those in night/alcohol accidents are probably close to an average cross-section of the pilot population in age and flying experience. That doesn't appear to be true of the day/alcohol pilots. Older, with more flying experience, this is clearly a different group as well as an easily identifiable one.

Moving on to the type accident and the airplanes involved in the two years covered by Figure 14, the biggest stack is assigned to buzzing and low-level aerobatics. Singles and twins are not separated in this graph because there are so few twins involved—only a 421, Aztec and Seneca in the case of buzzing accidents. The high incidence of J-3 Cubs in the buzzing column is interesting: more J-3's seem to wind up in drinking/buzzing accidents than in any other place. If we could separate the Cubs from their boozed-up buddies, at least we could save some of those fine old birds for another generation of pilots. Cubs aside, the airplanes in buzzing accidents seem slightly above average value when compared with the airplanes in the next highest column, uncontrolled descent. Those uncontrolled crashes are most often related to an inebriated pilot pressing on VFR in adverse weather, but in a few cases the poor pilot was so drunk that he simply lost control of the airplane in excellent weather.

Some lower alcohol levels are associated with buzzing accidents, but in a few the pilot was clearly drunk as a goat.

Pilot age is worth further consideration.

Automotively, the most likely participant in an alcohol-related accident is between twenty-five and thirty-five, single, and driving an older car. In airplanes, this group is involved in only a bit over one quarter of the accidents. In cars, drivers younger than twenty-five are in an ever-increasing number of alcohol-related accidents (especially since the drinking age has been lowered in many states) but this group hardly appears in the aviation problem.

The alcohol/age relationship is one example of how younger pilots must tend to have more respect for airplanes. Whereas they drive recklessly and are prone to drink and then drive with more gusto than the old bus can take, most must tend to put the prescribed time between bottle and airplane throttle. I suppose the alcohol/age relationship could also be used to argue that as we grow older we learn to better manage our drinking before driving, whereas flying after drinking even a small amount is not a skill that can be acquired.

BY CERTIFICATE

The distribution of alcohol-related accidents by pilot certificate has few surprises. There are few students, which is a reflection of the fact that students fly with more supervision. A student would not be likely to go to the airport wearing a few drinks, and even if the student did, the instructor would not be likely to let that student go flying in an airplane.

PURPOSE OF THE FLIGHT

In the course of one year, there was a single alcohol-related accident during a flight for hire. It was an instructional dual night flight with an inebriated flight instructor. A couple of accidents happened on business flights, and the rest occurred during pleasure and personal transportation flights. That is quite logical, and it perhaps dispels any thought that the businessman pilot would be very prone to this type of accident because of the alleged social pressures to imbibe heavily for business reasons before lunch, for example.

RESEARCH

There has been a considerable amount of research done on the alcohol subject, both in laboratories and in airplanes, and the conclusion is always what anyone could have guessed before the project started: Alcohol does have a very detrimental affect on a person's ability to fly an airplane. Any person who both flies and uses alcohol, and has ever given a minute's thought to the possible consequences of mixing the two, could probably come up with conclusions similar to any research.

Some things—personal experiences, perhaps—might tend to lead a few people astray, though. Some often feel sharper after they have had, say, one drink or even a few drinks. What about that? Why not fly?

In research done a number of years ago, the FAA tested psychomotor coordination on some subjects through the use of light panels controlled by hand levers and foot pedals. As signal lights indicated different light arrangements, the test subjects used hand and foot controls to arrange lights on a panel as suggested by the signal. Alcohol level was adjusted upward with brandy and downward with time. Careful records of performance were kept, and the conclusion was that there was no severe deterioration in performance with blood-alcohol levels associated with a little less than two ounces of good liquor or a couple of beers for a 160-pound person. The effect of that amount of alcohol was about the same as the slowdown in processes induced by eating a big lunch. Past that level, performance deteriorated rapidly in the test subjects.

ON THE OTHER HAND . . .

If you like it, contradiction is available in any area subjected to testing processes: A study conducted by a foreign air force offered a finding suggesting that alcohol doesn't really affect performance. This program was conducted in a simulator. The pilot flew a program sober, and then drank half of a small bottle of gin and flew the program again. He was in high spirits at this time, but did not appear intoxicated. After waiting a half hour, the pilot killed the bottle of gin, washed it down with a pint of beer, and then headed for the simulator again. He appeared intoxicated at this time, though his mental processes seemed relatively intact. After flying again, he slept for nine hours and then flew the program one more time, fuzzy head and all. In measuring his performance (in deviation from a ground track), they found that the pilot didn't do as well when sober as after a half bottle of gin. He improved even more after drinking the rest of the gin and the beer. The worst performance was the morning after.

That doesn't prove anything other than the fact that one pilot did okay in a simulator after having quite a bit to drink. It might, however, illustrate how some people lull themselves into thinking that it is okay to fly after drinking. Most of the pilots involved in alcohol-related accidents have some level of dependence on alcohol, and they are the type of people who search for reasons to justify the mixing of alcohol with any activity. The fact that a pilot can fly in a manner that seems satisfactory to him after consuming a large amount of alcohol might just be the straw. That pilot might indeed fly close to the line, but he might also fly into the ground while doing so. Or he might make an error in judgment that would result in a catastrophe.

TRY IT

If accident statistics and test results aren't enough, there is one thing the individual can do and one thing the individual can consider to prove that alcohol and airplanes don't mix: fly a simulator as you have a few. Fly the difficult problems. Fly the back course approaches and try partial panel: These are the things that make you think and reason as well as fly. Most any pilot will see a deterioration in ability.

Then consider all the letters you have written after having had a few drinks. Ever read them the next day before mailing them? Ever throw them away and start over? In an airplane you don't get to start over the next morning. The performance of the moment is the one that counts—no second chances.

HOW MUCH DISTANCE?

There is no rational argument to offer in favor of flying while influenced by alcohol. The real question, for those who both fly and drink, is in relation to the length of time that should be put between flying and drinking. The hangover is the prime question.

Go back to the test with that pilot with a foreign air force. His worst performance came the morning after the night before. He could actually do a better job of tracking while under the influence of quite a bit of alcohol than he could when suffering from the aftereffects. If you had to pick one condition or the other—under the influence or hung over—does that mean that the pilot could do a more effective job of operating an airplane safely while under the influence of alcohol than he could later on? I think not. A person might be able to command enough concentration to fly a tracking maneuver reasonably well while inebriated, but other things would likely be neglected. The reasoning and judgment processes would be more affected while under the direct influence than with a hangover.

Judgment is an important part of the alcohol v. flying question, too. Remember that while some of the accidents involve impairment or incapacitation in relatively normal phases of flight, most involve difficult situations created by the pilot, situations that probably would not have been created by a sober pilot.

I think it questionable that a pilot's judgment would be greatly affected by a hangover. If anything, the hangover might cause more caution. It is just not an adventuresome time in one's life, and certainly an airplane is not an attractive surrounding in which to nurse the ailment.

LASTING EFFECTS

There are some demonstrable effects of a hangover that will affect the visual and vestibular systems, those most closely associated with disorientation, long after any measurable alcohol is gone from the system. These systems can actually show the effects of alcohol for as long as twenty-four hours. The phenomenon might not matter in flying where the tendency to become disoriented isn't strong, but a relatively inexperienced or rusty IFR pilot making a takeoff at minimums eight hours after having several drinks could have a battle on his hands even though no alcohol remained in the bloodstream.

GUIDELINES

The FAA's rule is that we not fly while under the influence of alcohol or within eight hours after the consumption of any alcoholic beverage. The eight-hour part is crystal clear, but it might mislead some by suggesting that eight hours is a good average time to put between the last drink and the airplane, regardless of circumstances. As noted, there can be some lingering effect that would make it unwise to undertake some flight operations eight hours after even moderate drinking. There are also situations in which a pilot might still be under the influence more than eight hours after taking the last drink.

BIG BOTTLE

For example, consider a situation in which a 160-pound person consumes six drinks of 100 proof, 1½ ounces each, during a cocktail party that lasts from eight in the evening until midnight. That is quite a bit of alcohol, but spread over four hours after a heavy meal, it might not leave this person feeling that it had been a monumental drinking bout. And the person might feel it okay to go home, get some sleep, and fly at eight the next morning. It wouldn't be, though. There would still be measurable alcohol in the blood at eight the next morning. In fact, the alcohol wouldn't be metabolized until about ten.

At that point, at ten the next morning, it would be legal for the pilot to fly. But it might not be wise. Those who wish to guard against any hangover-induced hazard as well as the hazards of alcohol might well put eight hours between the time the alcohol is completely metabolized and flying. This isn't as restrictive as it might sound. For example, a 160-pound person can have three doubles (six ounces of 100 proof) between five and six in the evening and be eight hours on the other side at ten the next morning. If the takeoff is scheduled for seven, it would be best not to have doubles the evening before. If you don't want to fool with the mathematics, just abstain.

MATH

If you do want to understand the mathematics, base your calculations on the fact that two beers or two ounces of 100 proof whisky are metabolized by a 100-pound person in five hours. The relationship with weight is direct, so if you weigh 200 pounds, it'll take 2½ hours to metabolize two beers or two ounces of 100 proof. If you have four ounces and weigh 200, it'll take five hours. If you weigh 150 pounds and have three ounces, it'll take five hours. If you weigh 150 pounds and have six ounces, it'll take ten hours. It's all in direct proportion to body weight v. the amount of alcohol—100 pounds of body weight metabolizes two ounces of 100 proof or two beers every five hours. (If you drink 86 proof, you'll get rid of it in direct proportion to proof.) It should be noted that the alcohol in liquor consumed after eating is metabolized at a slower rate than the predinner, empty-stomach liquor. Its effects linger longer and are a good argument for skipping a nightcap the evening before a flight.

ALCOHOL v. ALTITUDE

It is often noted that the effect of alcohol increases with altitude. I once wrote something that contained a contradictory note on this. It related a test in which people with no alcohol and people with enough alcohol to induce a moderate effect were taken to 12,000 feet. In the experiment the alcohol caused the same relative deterioration in performance in the alcohol and the nonalcohol group. The point was disputed by some physicians interested in aviation. It was their feeling that all factors associated with drinking—fatigue, hangovers, curative drugs, heavy smoking, and the alcohol itself—lower altitude tolerance. Perhaps the part about "relative deterioration" is the key. The nonalcohol group started at sea level and suffered some deterioration, say, to eight on a scale of ten. The alcohol subjects didn't start at ten because of the alcohol. Perhaps they started at four and deteriorated to two. Each group might have dropped two points on a research scale, but the alcohol group might have gone from a coherent state to an incoherent state in so doing.

The argument about altitude is almost moot anyway. Most pilots who have accidents while under the influence don't fly at a high enough altitude for this to matter. It should be added, too, that oxygen is probably the best thing for freshening the mind when it's suspected that the effect of last evening's drink is making the morning fuzzy around the edges. Oxygen is much more effective than aspirin, and, in fact, aspirin increases a person's oxygen consumption and could contribute to lower altitude tolerance.

HOW MANY

The accident record gives us a picture of the accidents caused by a pilot's excessive drinking. There's no way to develop a theory on the number of accidents in which low alcohol amounts or a hangover might be a factor, but there are bound to be a fair number of these. If there are as many such accidents as there are accidents in which the pilot is under the active influence of alcohol, as determined by the NTSB, then over 10 percent of the fatal accidents might be considered alcohol-related. That makes it a large problem, and one to avoid with understanding.

MARIJUANA AND FRIENDS

There is little in the available accident data to link the use of marijuana and other illegal drugs to flying. For one thing, marijuana is apparently not detectable in the blood test that is conducted during autopsies. Some drugs are, and they show up occasionally. The government, though, must not tend to put much effort into linking possible drug involvement with airplane accidents. At least I had one file in which an FAA-conducted toxicological examination revealed nothing of consequence, but the local coroner's report indicated drug levels compatible with impairment. Local people suggested that the pilot had a history of drug-related legal problems, but this obviously suggested nothing to the accident investigator.

Marijuana is the most widely used drug, and in visiting with some people likely to use it, I found a widespread feeling that there is probably very little flying done by people while under the influence of marijuana. It's just not that type of thing. Where liquor often tends to excite the adventuresome spirit in people, the effects of marijuana are more related to love and visions than to things like airplanes. Some suggested that the effects come and go in such a definite manner that you just wouldn't consider doing something like flying an airplane while under the influence. Of course, these people could be looking at the situation through rose-colored glasses, and at some point we could wind up with an identified drug/flying problem. There's no doubt that flying while under the influence of drugs would be as dangerous as flying while under the influence of alcohol, so the two activities must be separated.

THE DEADLY SIDE

There does exist a very hazardous identified relationship between marijuana and flying. A relatively substantial number of accidents occur as general aviation airplanes are used to haul marijuana into and around the country. Some are weather accidents, and some are prompted by fuel exhaustion. There almost seems to be a correlation between the Mexican border, the range of average airplanes, and the location of the fuel exhaustion accidents. They must strive for nonstop deliveries.

The stakes are high in this type of operation, and the accidents are examples of the ultimate in pressure flying. There could be more money riding on the successful delivery of an old Lockheed full of grass than on the average daily flights of a fleet of bizjets. The illegal nature of the flights would only tend to increase the pilot's eagerness to get it over with and to avoid any unscheduled stops. The pilots in such accidents tend to have a pocketful of licenses and a logbook full of flying time, but this doesn't seem to get the old birds through the weather and to the destination. Nor does it serve to keep the airplane flying after all the fuel is gone. In a way, it is a shame that such mishaps have to be counted as general aviation accidents. They have their effect on the total record, by which the activity is judged, even though the flights are conducted for illegal purposes.

NOT BAD

I think the total record speaks rather well for people who fly. The involvement of alcohol and drugs in airplane accidents is clearly far less than is the case with automobiles, and we seem able to isolate most of the drinking and flying problems as ones related to people suffering from alcoholism.

As we manage our personal risks, this is an easy one to handle. Also, don't ever be reluctant to blow the whistle on someone you know who is unable to keep the alcohol or drugs separate from the airplane. It could be the greatest favor you might ever do for the person.

13 | Big Brother

In 1980, the FAA spent almost seventy dollars for every hour that was flown by civil aircraft in the United States. The money was procured from Congress, largely in the name of safety, and it is only natural to devote some thought to the effectiveness of alleged safety-related services that exceed the operating cost of most airplanes in the fleet.

To begin with, the FAA is not entirely to blame for its enormous budget. True, the FAA begs, but only Congress can produce the money. It flows very freely after major catastrophes. The Grand Canyon collision between two airliners in 1956 prompted the first real opening of the gates. The public's fear of falling after a collision was excited: "Do something." All Congress knew to do was spend money. The FAA took the money and set out to avoid another Grand Canyon collision. They were successful;

there hasn't been another case of two airliners colliding over the Grand Canyon—elsewhere, yes, but not there.

And so it has gone. Barn door after barn door has been closed after the horse has escaped. Airplanes have been certificated under rigorous government regulations only to develop flaws. Billions have been spent on the air traffic control system, yet there are still incidents and accidents within the system. Pilots have been burdened with more and more regulations and increased equipment requirements, yet they still fly airplanes into the ground. Each time some part of the system shows a weakness, the FAA is called on the carpet. Instant experts crawl out of the woodwork. Fingers are pointed, and finally something, anything, is done to close another barn door. If at any time Congress wanes in its enthusiasm for funding the FAA, you can almost imagine an empire builder clandestinely approaching Senator Claghorn at a party: "Okay, Senator, don't give us the money we want. But next time you fly, you might die. Don't forget that."

That is probably the way it will continue, too. Congress will appropriate, the FAA will spend, and there will always be some risk in aviation. There is no way to remove it all. The exercise on collision avoidance systems is a good example. The FAA knows that there will always be some collisions. The only way to eliminate the collision risk would be to let just one airplane fly at a time. Congress knows this, too, but nobody in government will look the flying public right in the eye and tell the truth: If you can't accept some risk of collision or other catastrophe, it's best just not to fly. There is no way to make it perfectly safe, but political considerations cause our government and the segments of industry that feed off such things to live the lie of offering instant regulatory or electronic solutions to all problems. The public seems to like it.

The closest approach to absolute safety has been the space program, with a perfect in-flight record to 1980. Consider, though, the amount of money spent for each hour flown in space and the restrictions on the activity. It came to a bunch more than the seventy dollars per hour spent by the FAA, and very few people get to participate.

THE SYSTEM

Most of the FAA's safety effort is directed toward air carrier flying. The traffic control system consumes most of the money and is designed primarily to control airliners flying between large cities. It is both effective and necessary for them, and the airlines are slaves to the system. With few exceptions, they are not allowed to fly unless participating in the air traffic control system.

The general aviation part of the air traffic control system and our use of it are only by-products of something that was developed to suit the needs of air carriers. It works pretty well, but it isn't an integral part of general aviation's fiber.

The effect of the air traffic control system on the users was well illustrated when there was a labor dispute a few years ago. The traffic control system's capacity was greatly reduced, and air carrier schedules turned to a shambles in many parts of the country. They wisely flew only as air traffic control service was available. General aviation managed quite well during the period, though, using a combination of VFR and IFR when available to get around. I think we learned that while a complete shutdown of the traffic control system would have an impact on general aviation, a high percentage of operations could still be conducted safely.

DIFFERENT CONCEPTS

Air carrier and general aviation are simply different concepts. The airlines are like railroads. Their activity is on a schedule and is concentrated on routes between few airports. The aircraft and crews have a marked sameness. General aviation is an almost entirely random operation. It flies between 10,000 airports in all types of airplanes. The pilots come in all levels of proficiency, from about zero up to the equal of the best airline crews.

Whereas air carrier operations are adaptable to regulation and regimentation, general aviation is the type of activity that defies regulation and would suffocate under strict regimentation. In fact, the only way the government might truly be able to influence the general aviation safety record is through restrictions. For example, we have continually noted that the accident rate in pleasure flying is higher than in business flying. The FAA might thus reason that it could improve the overall safety record by promulgating regulations that would decrease the amount of pleasure flying. Some of the ideas they have developed on mandatory equipment requirements strongly suggest that such a policy isn't foreign to the FAA's thinking.

THE BEST EXAMPLE

The difficulty of regulating safety in general aviation is best illustrated in the air taxi safety record. Air taxi has about the same fatal accident rate as business flying, yet air taxi is flown under much more stringent regulations.

Air taxi operators must have an FAA certificate plus an operations manual. If flight plans are not filed, the operator must have a procedure for locating the flight. Records must be kept on each flight. A pilot training program must be conducted, and detailed maintenance records must be kept. None of that applies to a pilot flying for business reasons.

Air taxi airplanes must have 100-hour inspections, whereas only annual inspections are required for business-use aircraft.

Operationally, any private pilot can fly for business. (Business flying is that not flown by professional flight crews. Operations that utilize hired crews are classed as corporate flying.) Air taxi pilot qualifications are much more demanding. For example, air taxi operation at night requires an instrument rating, and air taxi IFR operations require a pilot with 1,200 hours flying time. Additionally, either two pilots or an approved autopilot is required for IFR. There is a restriction on the use of single-engine aircraft for IFR air taxi.

There are pages of regulations on things like instrument check requirements, weather, flight time limitations, engine-out performance requirements for twins, and restrictions on single-engine IFR flying. None of these rules applies to business flying.

The airplanes flown in the two uses are similar, the same really, yet the relatively unregulated businessman has as good a safety record flying these airplanes as does the much more tightly regulated professional pilot flying air taxi. If you want to jump up a notch and consider corporate flying, that done by hired pilots, its record is twice as good as air taxi, even though this flying is also subjected to much less regulation than air taxi.

MORE IS BETTER?

The governmental answer to this has been more regulation for air taxi operators. It probably will only serve to put some of them out of business, though, and probably will not help the safety record. In reality, the air taxi safety record is set by factors other than regulation. It is set by the type of operations and by the individual pilot's survival instincts. You could take the special rules for air taxi, wad them up, and toss them in the can, and the air taxi record probably wouldn't change appreciably. They would probably do as well operating under the same rules that apply to business and pleasure flying.

Thinking back to some of the accident causes does a lot to explain why excessive regulation doesn't do much for a general aviation activity such as air taxi flying.

RULES v. WEATHER

We noted that most of the IFR accidents involve premature arrivals—flight into the ground before reaching the airport on an IFR approach. Sure, there are rules on the subject, but the rules help only the pilot who wants to be helped. Those who wish to fudge can do so, often while almost convincing themselves that they aren't really doing anything wrong or illegal.

A lot of the night IFR accidents might not even involve a violation of any rule. In many the pilot's error is in succumbing to a visual illusion. No law against that. The pilot might properly stay at the minimum descent altitude until the runway lights or approach lights are in sight, and then fly into the ground while looking at these lights in the distance.

In other weather accidents, a pilot might start out with everything properly VFR for the flight only to encounter IFR conditions. At that time his brain, not a rule, will save the day.

SINGLE-ENGINE, FOR EXAMPLE

Then look at the FAA's restrictions on single-engine IFR operations by air taxi operators. It is so restricted that few operators bother even to try it. Yet the record in business flying, where single-engine airplanes are widely used for IFR flying, offers no reason for any curb on this type of activity. In one recent year, there was not one fatal engine-failure-related accident in single-engine airplanes used for business flying. You can almost sense the governmental reasoning behind a rule like this, though. Even if it involves no true and undue risk, an air taxi accident following an engine failure in a single could bring the ceiling down upon a bureaucrat's head. Have accidents in airplanes with two engines, though, and that can appear as "one of those things—we did our best on the rules."

When contemplating the regulation of air taxi flying, we can almost charge it all off as something that the FAA feels it must do in order to show an attempt at a higher level of safety where paying passengers are involved.

THE LAW v. WEATHER

Looking at the total picture, the problem of the pilot without an instrument rating proceeding VFR into adverse weather conditions appears one that might logically be expected to respond to regulation. The FAA is aware, too, that a substantial reduction in the number of this type of accident would lead to a marked improvement in the accident record, but so far they have not been able to develop anything of substance.

Some years ago, the FAA decided that limited instrument training for private pilots would help reduce weather accidents. The reasoning was that a pilot should at least have limited ability to fly by reference to the gauges so he could survive long enough to call for help, or to make a turn and fly back out of the inclement weather. The trouble is the smattering of instrument training doesn't stick unless the pilot follows a methodical proficiency maintenance program. What little ability is developed in the program tends to desert pilots when most needed. Also, it could have a negative effect by inducing weather-related boldness in certain pilots. There is nothing wrong with some instrument training for all private pilots, but I doubt if much value could be proven except in cases where the pilot moves on into real instrument training.

MINIMUMS

The FAA has worked with some legal weather minimums in an effort to improve the situation. It abolished Special VFR at night, and this has probably prevented some accidents. However, only a small percentage of the airports are in control zones, where Special VFR is applicable, and pilots are free to fly VFR at night with one-mile visibility from any airport that doesn't have a control zone. So there are still plenty of legal opportunities for the pilot who wishes to tempt fate in the dark.

The night weather problem related to pilots on VFR flights might respond favorably to some adjustment in the regulations on minimum weather. Proportionately a very high percentage of the weather accidents occur at night. Going to the rules, we find that the Special VFR prohibition at night is *the only* regulation on VFR minimums that differentiates between daylight and dark. Certainly there is more than that to consider between day and night marginal VFR flying, and the FAA might eventually work in this fertile field. There's nothing wrong with night VFR, but logic certainly suggests that you need much better weather for it than for day VFR.

DAY VFR

Whereas the FAA has never created even a mild rumble about adjusting the night VFR weather minimums, they have made noises about the overall VFR minimums. They generally meet with opposition from the users. The present minimums can be lethal in areas of rough terrain, but they do seem okay in flat country. Should the FAA place restrictions on the pilot flying in Kansas, which is flat as a billiard table, because people persist in flying into the relatively small but very adequate hills over in Arkansas? No way. The flexibility of VFR must remain, but we must do a better job of training pilots on the reasonable use of these minimums.

At an FAA/user meeting, one weather-related rule the FAA proposed to change was about IFR takeoff minimums. Air carrier and air taxi operations had takeoff minimums, but these did not apply to Part 91 operations, basically those not conducted for hire. This had been bothering the FAA for years, and they had unsuccessfully made the proposal to put Part 91 pilots under the takeoff minimum rule a number of times. This was another attempt.

There was discussion of the proposal, and finally the general aviation people in the audience started pressing the FAA for documentation, for solid reasons why the rule change should be made. Neither the FAA nor the National Transportation Safety Board had any justification to offer. Many logical reasons not to make the rule were offered, and finally an FAA person thought up one reason in favor: It would simplify the controller's lot by letting him deny takeoff clearances during periods of low visibility on a uniform basis. Hopefully, as regulatory changes are sought that will improve the safety record, the government will do better than that.

THE THUNDERSTORM RULE

Thus far, the government has not made any rules about not flying through thunderstorms, even though the results of such an attempt are at times rather tragic. It has been contemplated, though, with the NTSB once suggesting that air traffic controllers be given the authority to deny takeoff or landing clearance when thunderstorms menace the airport, departure, or approach paths.

There is some logic to a thought like that, and perhaps it would prevent accidents. Surely the local police have the authority to close a road that is inundated or otherwise affected, and this would only be an aeronautical parallel to such a rule. The rule could also cause chaos as airplanes of different weight and handling characteristics moved through an area of convective turbulence. If the controller

were to be saddled with this authority and a Cessna Skyhawk pilot reported severe turbulence on final, what would
the controller do about the jumbo jet following along? If
the airport were to be closed to the jumbo because of observed precipitation on radar and the Skyhawk pilot's report, the jumbo might be unnecessarily delayed. On the
other hand, if the controller decided to factor the report for
airplane size and let the jumbo keep on coming and it had
an accident, then things would be bad indeed for that controller.

Thunderstorms are dynamic and rather unpredictable
characters, and I suspect that they will forever defy regulation. Again, understanding is the key.

VFR NOT RECOMMENDED

In another weather-related effort, the FAA instituted a
program to make recommendations about not undertaking
VFR flights. When the flight service station specialist deems
that the weather is marginal or below VFR, the briefing is
concluded with the statement "VFR not recommended."

Unless the pilots take it with understanding and a grain
of salt, this program could have a detrimental effect on
safety for several reasons.

To begin with, if a pilot is deterred a few times, only to
note that the weather was actually pretty good, that pilot is
no longer likely to pay attention to any admonishment
about weather from the FSS. And when a specialist does
not say the magic words "VFR not recommended," a gul-

lible pilot might take that as an indication that VFR *is* recommended by none other than the U.S. government. If the weather turns out to be bad, the pilot could be in for a rude awakening.

NO-NO

The FAA surely does have the wisdom to know that it can't solve the weather accident problem with rules and admonishments. The key is in pilot education and improved dissemination of weather information. Pilot education is the most important part, too, and the FAA actually took a step backward in this area not long ago with the institution of plain-language weather briefings. This is a real kindergarten delivery of weather information. Actually, the FAA should dispense only information and should work at developing an educational system that insures that every pilot knows as much or more about meteorology than the people now manning the flight service stations. The person flying the airplane is the person who must make the decisions.

STALL/SPIN

There's no effective way to write a rule that would keep pilots from inadvertently stalling airplanes at the wrong time, so the FAA has had to rely on educational programs in working to reduce stall/spin accidents. In one way, this has taken on some aspects of a comic opera.

The FAA's flight instructor revalidation teams, groups that traveled the country conducting seminars, tended to reinvent the wheel occasionally. That was perhaps done in the rather common educator's effort to develop something tricky that can be used to show that the educator is smarter than the student. In one such move, they decided that when power is variable and available, the elevator *always* controls altitude and power always controls airspeed. Flight instructors sat through years of that, with the FAA people making snide remarks about people who disagreed. (Langewiesche, Kershner, and Collins were frequently mentioned.) The FAA stall recovery became a matter of putting the nose on the horizon with the elevator (hold altitude) and giving it full throttle (make airspeed).

Then, suddenly, the FAA changed, or at least it contradicted itself. An advisory circular appeared that plainly stated that the elevator controls airspeed and power controls altitude. Why the apparent change? Perhaps the FAA saw the light. The safety message for pilots is to carefully contemplate dramatic and controversial pronouncements on flying technique regardless of who makes them.

AIRCRAFT CERTIFICATION

The FAA's role in aircraft certification and in the licensing of individual airplanes after they are built is the subject of frequent debate. The procedure is for the FAA to make rules and set standards under which airplanes must be designed and built. Then the FAA monitors design and building to ensure that the manufacturers are living up to the letter (and the intent) of the law. The FAA does not approve design, nor do they approve each airplane that is built. This horrifies some—especially those who feel that the government should project itself more into every element of our society. But failures attributable to this method of certification and approval account for a minuscule percentage of the serious accidents.

The FAA is active in the design process to the point of setting special conditions for some airplanes (for example, when the FAA feels the airplane has an unusual feature that is not adequately covered by existing rules), and FAA engineering test pilots do fly new airplanes during the certification process. Often they make a contribution to design; but at times the manufacturers feel like the FAA pilots are there to harass them. For example, on one single, the FAA test pilot held up certification because an abrupt application of full power—as the airplane was being dived at the red-line speed—resulted in a slight overrev of the engine before the prop governor adjusted rpm to the red line. This will happen in virtually all airplanes with constant speed props, which fact was finally used to convince the FAA that this one was okay.

Those who feel that the FAA should take more part in the certification process cite examples of the DC-10 engine pylon problem, the Cessna Conquest tail problem, and the grounding and numerous airworthiness directives on the Piper Tomahawk as concrete examples of why the FAA needs to be more in on the act.

Would it have helped? It is highly likely that the problems with the three airplanes mentioned would have been there, and would have been just as severe even with tripled or quadrupled FAA involvement in the design process. The FAA followed the development of these airplanes, as they do of all airplanes, and the FAA knew what was going into each. In the DC-10 and Conquest, the problem was not that the original design did not meet the FAA specification —which would have been all any FAA engineer might have insisted on had one been looking over the shoulder of each McDonnell Douglas or Cessna engineer. The probable causes had more to do with relationships—between design and maintenance in one case and between the tail and vibration in the other. The Tomahawk was a matter of a new airplane developing a number of small problems that were related as much to production as to design.

Consider, too, that design problems are very expensive to the people who build airplanes. If an engine or tail separates, there are lawsuits, lost sales, and expensive fixes for the airplane. And while it is hardly as painful to the builder as to the occupants of the airplane, money does motivate.

Even a massive increase in the FAA's role in the certification of aircraft design and individual aircraft would not lead to a meaningful improvement in the safety record. There just aren't that many related accidents to prevent. And more FAA involvement would almost certainly have a lot to do with cost. One has only to look at our experience with military airplanes to sample the delights of more government involvement in airplane design. Cost overruns, structural problems, engine problems, systems problems are all found there. The simple fact is that every airplane is a compromise, and if you get too many people involved in the compromise there's likely to be no utility left in the airplane when it is completed. Those of us who fly just have to accept the very small risk attendant to the fallibility of the engineering profession. And it is important that we not spend a lot of time making smoke over something that has historically caused few accidents—certification in this case —while neglecting the real problem area, the pilot and his relationship with the airplane.

BIENNIAL FLIGHT REVIEW

The FAA took a step toward exposing pilots to a periodic examination of their skills with the biennial flight review rule. This was enacted over the protests of some, but the fact that the flight review is conducted by flight instructors, not government inspectors, quieted some of the opposition. Also, there's no way to fail. If a pilot doesn't measure up to the instructor's expectations, the next step is to continue the review process until up to snuff. The continuation can be with the instructor who declined to sign off a successful completion, or it can be with another instructor. The rules are not specific on what should be covered in a biennial.

Has this done anything to improve the safety record? It is hard to tell, but it is necessary to acknowledge that it certainly hasn't made the record worse.

If there's weakness it's because the instructors of our land haven't done a very uniform job with the biennial flight review; the result is perhaps not as much improvement in the safety record as might have been possible.

To get a feel for the quality of reviews, one pilot went to

three different places for a biennial. One gave him a real onceover lightly—a quick review of the rules and a short flight wrapped it up. An old timer at a small strip gave him quite a workout—two separate flight and ground sessions; one flight session was on a wild and windy day. And at a big city flight school he got something in between. One thing is certain: the old timer knew a lot more about his flying skills and knowledge of the rules than the other two. And he charged less.

The pilot has a lot to do with the quality of a biennial. Instead of seeking out the most difficult or expensive review, human nature probably leads most to the place where it's the easiest and the least expensive. That's too bad, because the biennial is really a minimum exposure to recurrent training and checking. If all pilots would seek out a tough check *annually*, things would probably improve a bit.

One of the hardest things to learn about a pilot is the quality of his judgment. You can't touch this on a biennial, and once past basic flying technique, judgment is the single most important ingredient for safe flying. A pilot might look good because he can take off and land, fly instruments with some precision, and operate the airplane in a manner that always keeps it a safe distance away from the typical stall/spin scenario. But does the pilot have good enough judgment to keep his nose out of thunderstorms, to flee ice at the first sign, to retreat and land instead of continuing VFR into adverse weather, to avoid buzzing and booze, and to make the other good decisions that make the difference between a safe and a dangerous aviator? The biennial will never shed light on those things, but, like safety seminars, it can be a vehicle for convincing the pilot that the wage of poor judgment is death.

THE LEDGER

The fact that aviation is more or less self-regulating is evident when the number of violations processed by the FAA is compared with the total number of accidents. Accidents tend to outnumber violations, and when you consider that a lot of the violations are filed after a pilot has had an accident, it is even more evident that the airplane itself handles a lot of the punishment. That isn't to belittle the FAA's enforcement effort. They are alert and prosecute vigorously when the occasion arises. Airplanes aren't like automobiles, though, and many of the violations such as an inadvertent entry into instrument conditions, come to a swift and accidental conclusion before a fed with a ticket book can enter the picture.

EQUIPMENT

The feds require us to equip our airplanes with certain devices if we are to do certain things. Some of these requirements contribute to safety; others are more a form of harassment. Encoding altimeters, for example, are devices that make the airplane more compatible with the air traffic control system, but their contribution to safety is not great. In fact, if you consider the things that pilots buy voluntarily, those that are not required by law, such as DME, autopilots, flight directors, redundant nav/com systems, and weather radar systems, you will see that contribution to safety by those items probably far outstrips the contribution of the hardware items that are required or are being advanced as possible requirements to mesh with a complicated system of positive control of air traffic.

BIG MONEY

In looking to prevent collisions through the imposition of control and the spending of money, the FAA has long favored control towers. Indeed, a study revealed that relatively low-activity airports with control towers were virtually collision-free over a period of years. Thus, one might reason, the extension of control tower service should contribute to safety. How about a tower at the 840 uncontrolled airports in the United States that combine to account for two-thirds of all flight operations and 73 percent of the midair collisions? If experience is valid, it would cut the collision hazard at those airports, but the cost would be $17 million *for each collision prevented.* As we look toward solutions for safety problems, they must be affordable. There is certainly some question there.

So it seems that no matter what our government does

through the FAA and through other agencies such as the NTSB, no breakthrough in general aviation safety is imminent or possible. And while a government role in aviation is very necessary, the record shows that this role could be diminished without any adverse effect on the safety potential of the activity.

14 | The Pilot/Airplane/ Accident Triangle

As we explore the accident record as well as history and the various things that are related to flying safely, it is continually noted that the pilot, the complex human, is the strength, the weakness, and the determiner of success. The federal aviation regulations recognize this with the following: "The pilot in command of an aircraft is directly responsible for, and is the final authority as to, the operation of the aircraft."

On the surface, it might appear that a person's behavioral traits in other areas could mirror the ability to accept that total responsibility and to manage risks in flying. It does not always work that way, though.

I know a lot of people who tend to drive recklessly: They speed, drive after having a bit much to drink, and generally operate cars in an unsafe manner. But when near an airplane, their demeanor changes. The aeronautical operation becomes a calculated plot against risks. The planning is methodical and the decisions are conservative. The execution is precise. Not one corner is cut.

On the other hand, some people who are extremely cautious in their daily lives take chances in airplanes you almost wouldn't believe. They drive like little old ladies, eat health foods, go to the doctor at the first sign of a stomachache, and have a fire-detector system at home and life jackets for all on the boat. Aeronautically, though, they refuse to invest any money in proficiency flying, and they have the airplane maintained by the low bidder. They fly when fatigued, continually tempt the elements, and steadfastly refuse to get an instrument rating. They flaunt the proven trouble areas and generally use the airplane in a high-risk manner. Speak to such a person about this, and the response might come with a sneer, as if the pilot feels that nobody should question his right to kill himself in an airplane.

Responsibility and risk management in flying are very individual affairs that may or may not be affected by other things. Also, the responsibility part is often a difficult thing to grasp in a time when the government is trying to become a bigger factor in our lives. Some feel that they are provided with a GI umbrella and that there must either be no risk or that risk must be managed by government in every area. The politicians will continue to debate that in many relationships, but there is no debate in aviation. It is impossible to assume responsibility or manage aeronautical risks from afar. Flying is an individual, John Wayne activity. What happens is determined by the pilot. If the pilot can't take the full responsibility, and cut it, trouble is bound to follow. Nobody can hold the pilot's hand. Nobody can fly the airplane for a pilot or cover up for any mistakes that are made by the pilot.

That all sounds a touch on the preachy side, but it is true, important, and the accident record provides an unlimited supply of examples to use in supporting the theory.

WEATHER

When checking weather, some pilots listen to a briefer, ask a few questions, and then take the product that someone else created in a few minutes and bet all the blue chips on it for hours. One such pilot said bitterly that there was no chance of thunderstorms mentioned in a weather briefing, yet he flew into a cell three hours later and had quite an interesting few minutes. The pilot criticized the person who gave him a weather briefing, but he should have looked into a mirror. The pilot should have continued checking the weather en route and continually reevaluated the decision to go. Any number of things would have informed him of the upcoming problem, but, no, he sat and waited for someone else to do his work, to tell him of the storm ahead.

DOOMED FROM THE BEGINNING

In many weather accidents, it is apparent that a pilot must have been driven into a precarious position by an almost blind obsession to get somewhere. This is illustrated in both

VFR and IFR accidents. The pilot might continue VFR into adverse weather conditions, or, if IFR, might descend below an altitude in an attempt to fudge on minimums. These are highly individual deeds, prompted only by the pilot's personal devil-on-shoulder. They have to be the result of doing something without regard for the possible consequences.

As we critique our own flying, it is important to analyze all situations in which a decision might be influenced by other than aeronautical factors. For example, the desire to get back home from a trip, sometimes called "get-home-itis," is a strong influence that we should recognize. Personally, I have long noted that I am more prone to cancel the first leg of a trip, the outbound leg, than I am to cancel the last leg, the one that returns me to the warmth of my own fireplace. Perhaps there is a greater reward to returning home than there is to going away on a business trip, and I am willing to accept a bit more risk in return for the reward. I try to convince myself that isn't the case, that only aeronautical factors are considered, but when I look at the record, at the trips canceled over the years, I find some guilt.

A compulsion to get somewhere in the airplane is a frequent activator of the domino theory, too. Fly on to the destination even though the weather is perhaps below minimums. Then start the approach based on wishful thinking. Next, at the minimum descent altitude, descend an extra hundred feet, then another hundred. Maybe the domino crushes the airplane as a result of this transgression; maybe it doesn't. Even if it doesn't, a seed is planted: next time.

DETERMINED FELLOW, HE WAS . . .

A pilot with a fresh license illustrated the domino theory in action as he tried to shoot an instrument approach on a pleasure trip. The airplane and the situation were both a bit over the pilot's head, and the approach was missed even though the weather was quite a bit above minimums. Then, as the pilot came around to try again, the weather got a bit worse. The second approach was also missed, and even though there was some further deterioration in the weather, the pilot opted to try for a third approach. He flew into the ground on this one, and the cause was deemed to be a descent below the decision height without the runway in sight. That might fit the computer, but the cause was really the pilot's failure to recognize after two missed approaches, two chances, that he wasn't up to the situation. It was a personal decision that he had to make. Giving up meant that a rented airplane would have had to be flown back home and the rental paid without the mission being accomplished. So near, yet so far. Try again. Nothing in the rules against it. No help on the decision. Gamble and lose.

LIMITATIONS OR CAPABILITIES?

Some would suggest that this pilot didn't know his limitations. That is a bad choice of words, though, and when the preacher in a safety seminar pounds the podium, raises his voice, and says, "Know your limitations" with evangelistic fervor, I'm always tempted to ask where they are printed. On my Jockey shorts? An airplane's limitations are printed out in black and white, but people don't really have limitations. It is better to think in terms of capabilities: "I, as a pilot, am capable of shooting that ILS approach." Then, "I, as a pilot, just missed that ILS approach in above minimum conditions so I am apparently not capable of landing here today and had best go home, even though it means a lot of money for nothing."

CIRCUMSTANCES

Circumstances related to individuals are often closely related to accidents. And some things recur so frequently that we almost come to think of them as accident causes rather than circumstances surrounding the mishaps.

Flying for pleasure or personal transportation is a prime example of a circumstance that is strongly related to accidents. The record here is much worse, very much worse, than in business, corporate, instructional, air taxi, or agricultural flying. It only takes a little reflection to see why.

A person using an airplane for personal transportation might be pressured to get back from a trip in time for work. Or there might be some reluctance to cancel for fear of losing face with family or friends. And often the pilot flying for personal reasons isn't as well trained as the pilot flying for business reasons. Nor might his airplane be as well equipped or maintained. The pleasure pilot pays for flying with after-tax dollars, which are a lot harder to come by than the before-tax dollars that the business user spends for his equipment, maintenance, proficiency flying, and perhaps even his training. Money can't buy safety, but at times failure to spend it can increase risk—especially in the training, proficiency, and maintenance areas.

PLAY

In local pleasure and recreational flying, we find many accidents that must be charged purely to playfulness on the part of an individual. Some can be charged to ignorance or poor technique, and many can be charged to showing off. There is a possible/impossible point in each and every thing that we do with airplanes, and the temptation to paw at the line between the two is strong when the airplane is being used to impress someone, to prove a point, or as an outlet for exhibitionism. To do these things is both fraught with peril and a highly individual decision.

NOT NECESSARY

It shouldn't be necessary to accept an increase in risk based simply on the tax status of a flight—business or pleasure. However, there is plenty of experience in other areas to show that this is something that might be expected. In automobile accidents, for example, almost 30 percent of the people killed are between fifteen and twenty-four years old. That is an age when a car is more of an outlet, a toy, than a means to an end. Also, the automotive death rate is from two to three times higher at night, when the car is more often used for pleasure or personal transportation than for business and humdrum uses such as commuting and grocery shopping. Alcohol is a factor in about half the automobile accidents—a strong reason why the car is more lethal when used at night, for fun.

Do consider the automotive experience when reading of the relationship between pleasure and personal transportation uses and general aviation accidents. The higher accident rate that we see here must be a natural thing, based on individual behavior, and it might be expected in any activity. It in no way means that a pilot flying for pleasure cannot use an airplane as safely as the business pilot. It only means that the pleasure pilot must accept the same constraints that seem naturally to keep the business pilot from doing the things that involve high risk. Difficult, perhaps, and as individuals we'll probably never fly as safely when flying for fun as we do when droning along, straight and level, in hot pursuit of nothing more than the almighty dollar.

FROM THE START

Business or monkey business, there is often a clear relationship between an accident and the pilot's actions right before takeoff. Preflight covers a lot more territory than kicking the tires, squirting the sumps, checking the fuel and oil, and flying away. Those are the mechanical items; when realistic thought is not put into assessing the total picture, an accident can follow along very shortly.

This can be clearly illustrated when examining accidents related to weight, balance, and density altitude. The circumstances might put the pilot at a small airport on a hot day with a big load. That is, incidentally, a more frequent happening in pleasure flying than, for example, business flying, and the circumstances offer the pilot the opportunity of having one hell of a bad accident. Prevention would be found only in something the pilot might do *before* attempting the takeoff. Preflight action would be the only salvation.

Calculations might show that the takeoff would be impossible, at worst, or very close, at best. By making the calculations, the pilot would clear the first hurdle. The second hurdle would be recognition of the message. The third hurdle would be enough of a change in the circumstances to make the takeoff possible. Waiting until the cool of the late afternoon or morning might do it. Leaving some fuel out and planning a stop at the nearest large airport might do the trick. Wise pilots have been known to take passengers out of a small strip one at a time in a shuttle operation to a nearby larger airport. Then the whole group can fly together from that larger airport. Whatever is done is up to the pilot. Nobody is likely to make any suggestions or offer any ideas. And if the pilot elects to try an impossible mission, the passengers will probably go along.

LOTS OF CHANCES

Flying gives us a lot of chances, but we have to find and take advantage of those chances. This is true in the mechanical sense as well as in areas affected by weather or airplane performance.

Procrastination is probably the most common human failure when it comes to mechanical items. I found a good example of this when operating my Cessna Skyhawk, designed for 80-octane fuel, on low-lead 100-octane fuel, which happened to be the only thing available to use. The problems associated with using 100-octane fuel in 80-octane engines were becoming legendary by the time my airplane had 500 hours on it, and I had my first lesson at about that time.

The airplane had just had a 100-hour inspection but was not running as smoothly as it should. A fast check revealed that the bottom spark plug in the number 4 cylinder was terribly fouled. The shop put a new plug in and dismissed the event with a "that-happens-all-the-time" attitude. I left on a trip, and an hour into the flight the engine started running rough again. The nearest airport was selected for a landing, and there I met a more cautious mechanic. He pulled the bottom plug from number 4, noted that it was terribly fouled again, and said that the cylinder had best come off to see what was causing the problem. It was full of lead deposits from the 100-octane fuel, and these deposits were breaking loose and fouling the bottom plug.

SHORT MEMORY

Only a few months later, I started having plug-fouling problems with the number 2 cylinder. In fact, it fouled both
plugs once, and a four-cylinder engine running on three
cylinders is on the far side of what you might call a rough
running engine. It attracts attention in a hurry. And you
would think that I would have learned by this time and
would have promptly had the number 2 cylinder removed
and checked for a cause. But, no, I convinced myself this
was different, changed plugs, and kept on going. And I
changed them again and again, and finally wised up and
decided that the cylinder had to come off. I think I finally
learned that when plugs foul once, be suspicious. When
they foul twice, have the cylinder removed and checked to
see what is going on.

The same requirement for basic suspicion of mechanical
problems holds true in all areas. For example, I read of a
pilot who had a great deal of difficulty starting one engine
on a twin, but finally got it going and promptly taxied out
and made an intersection takeoff. As the airplane was passing the end of the runway, the engine that had been reluctant to start decided to become temperamental again and it
just quit cold. A very serious accident followed. If the pilot
had been supersuspicious, he would have had the engine
checked before the flight. Allowing for a normal amount of
procrastination, one might have to let the pilot assume that
the start was hard because of something like a vapor lock

and that once the engine was running it would be okay. Even then, a mild suspicion probably would have saved the pilot by prompting him to start the takeoff from the end of the runway instead of from an intersection and to verify power output carefully before takeoff.

PILOT v. TYPE

Our relationship with different airplanes involves individual and responsible discipline because rules require a bare minimum in this area. For example, I stay legally current for passenger carrying in all prop single-engine land, single-engine sea, and prop-driven multiengine land airplanes weighing under 12,500 pounds simply by making three landings (or splashes, in the case of the seaplane) in any one example airplane in each of the three categories every ninety days. Three landings in a Cessna 150 and I'm current in a Bonanza; three in an Apache and I'm current in a King Air; three in a Lake Amphibian and I'm current in a Helio Courier on floats—legally current, that is (as the rules were written in 1980), and as has been noted before, all that's legal isn't safe.

While we might look at a checkout or practice some flying in an airplane before leaving on a trip as an admission of a lack of skill or proficiency, the checkout and some practice go hand in hand with flying safely.

There are numerous ways to delude ourselves as we fly different airplanes, too. For example, a pilot with instrument, single, and multiengine ratings is free to fly IFR in both single and multiengine airplanes. And I've seen pilots get their instrument rating in a a single-engine airplane "because it is easier" and then attempt IFR operations in a twin without any additional practice or training. There is a risk involved in multiengine IFR flying by a pilot with only single-engine IFR experience, and accidents and incidents prove this quite frequently. There's more to distract in the twin, and a pilot should be trained and current on handling the distractions while operating in the IFR environment.

BURGEONING QUESTION

As a result of some pertinent accidents, there has been a lot of talk about who is really responsible for qualifying the pilots who fly different airplanes. An incident I overheard on an air traffic control frequency outlines the problem.

The pilot was flying a Cessna 340, and when he first called the center to air-file an IFR flight plan, he identified his point of departure at a small resort area sod strip with which I was familiar. The strip is about 3,000 feet long, and the day was a hot one. As the pilot filed his flight plan, the fuel and number of people on board strongly suggested that the airplane was at or over gross weight when it left the small sod strip. I only wondered if he understood the risk involved in operating a twin in such a manner. Strike one.

As the pilot continued, there was a great deal of hesitation in his approach to the situation and quite a bit of misunderstanding between the pilot and the controller. The weakness was all on the part of the pilot. He read a clearance back incorrectly and then changed altitude after asking for a change, but before being cleared for the change by the controller. Strike two.

Then the inevitable thunderstorms lined up across the pilot's path. The airplane had weather radar on board, but the pilot was clearly not trained in its use. As the storms were approached, the pilot's continuing requests for information turned into plaintive pleading: "Please lead me through." It was a sad, pitiful exercise. It was quite obvious that while the pilot might have been capable of taking off and landing the 340, he was certainly not qualified to operate the airplane as it was meant to be operated. He seemed to survive that day's activity, probably with the help of an autopilot, but another day might well get him.

WHOSE FAULT?

Who is responsible for a situation like that? The airframe manufacturer? The airplane salesman? The FAA? The insurance company? They all have a role in putting the pilot in the left front seat of the airplane, but the pilot alone has to bear the responsibility of operating the airplane, so it stands to reason that the pilot should assure that he is capable of doing so. The man had to have enough sense to make the money to buy the airplane, so surely it would be reasonably easy to convince him that it takes more than the legal (or insurance company) minimum to fly the airplane without wiping himself and his family out in one stroke. Aviation suffers through a lot of tragedies caused by situations like this; a substantial number of them are very predictable, and the solution is going to have to be found in individual understanding of the risks involved.

NOT COMPATIBLE

It is true, too, that some people probably are just not compatible with airplanes. It is hard to tell an intelligent person that he or she should just push off from an activity like flying, but it occasionally needs to be done. Just as every person in the world is not cut out to be a doctor, lawyer, politician, or great lover, every person in the world is not cut out to be an airplane pilot. And when a person who doesn't adapt keeps trying, the result is frustration at best and an accident at worst.

How can you tell when a person should quit trying to master the airplane? The answer is both difficult and a highly individual matter. I recall one person I was trying to teach to fly a number of years ago and the mental torment the man was subjecting himself to while trying to learn to fly. Landings were seemingly beyond his grasp. Try as he would, he couldn't find the ground with the little airplane after twenty-five hours of dual. He would end each flight in a fit of frustration and vow never to come back. Then, in a few days, he would call for another lesson and we would try again.

Late one day when the air was smooth and hardly a breath of wind was stirring, he finally produced a string of reasonable landings. I seized the opportunity and told him this was it—first solo. I left him alone in the airplane and walked over to the side of the runway. He took off without hesitation, flew the pattern, and then made a successful if not smooth landing. The fellow refused to shoot another solo landing, though. In fact, to my knowledge he never flew an airplane again. He had soloed, and he left happy. I was glad that I had been able to solo him and was relieved that he quit flying because he would have always been a marginal pilot.

I've often thought about that person and have tried to develop a mental picture of a personality that would lead to such a problem. He was a smart guy, and the only characteristic I could isolate had to do with his inability to think rapidly and then make his hands and feet do the required work. His decisions were usually good, he could usually tell me what he had done incorrectly, but he was incapable of patching things up with his own hand. I guess he was a procrastinator in all things, and procrastination doesn't have much of a role in landing airplanes.

METHODICAL AND CURRENT

Once we are up to speed in airplanes in general and one airplane in particular, a methodical approach to flying remains quite important. I got a reminder of this when flying a rather sophisticated airplane with another pilot recently. We had flown the airplane earlier and were headed out for another round. The weather was quite bad, with rain and thundershowers throughout the area. The clearance finally came through, and when it did I ran my mental "instruments, controls, fuel, and trim" checklist, pulled out on the runway, and launched.

We had been off and climbing for about five minutes when the other pilot looked over to my side and said, "I guess we should have those alternators on." In our preoccupation with getting started, watching the weather, and getting a clearance, we had missed that part of the checklist. The embarrassing thing was the annunciator panel: Two bright lights were telling us that the alternators were not on all the while, and neither of us noticed them.

PRACTICE MAKES, WELL . . .

Practice is an important part of flying safely. Oh, I don't mean that we should go out and practice chandelles, S-turns, and other such basic training maneuvers. Instead, we should practice things that are difficult, that require precision, and that are practical. An IFR favorite of mine is partial panel under the hood. Covering the artificial horizon and direction gyro simulates a failure of the vacuum system—a very real possibility—and the challenge is to shoot an ILS approach to minimums with things in this state. It's hard work, it takes some practice to stay current, but it is rewarding in the sense that it offers in my single-engine airplane the redundancy that I might get from dual vacuum pumps in a twin. I also like to practice spot landings. It's surprising how widely you miss the mark when rusty on these, and, again, skill at spot landings offers a form of redundancy. Engines seldom quit, but if one ever did, the ability to put the airplane precisely where you want it would be quite handy.

It is often tempting to practice only the things that we do well, but the opposite is much more useful. Practicing to learn something contributes a lot more to flying safely than practicing to exhibit perfection. And practicing is a highly individual matter. We set the time, the place, and the format.

DOUBLE REVERSE

It was noted earlier that airplanes don't do well at keeping secrets. There are instances, though, where something that is not apparent can surface as pilots adjust to a new airplane coming into the fleet. Such situations are worth exploring because, in retrospect, a modicum of logic and reason might have prevented a lot of trouble.

The Twin Comanche example that was noted is a classic example of this. People buy and use light twins because they feel there is a safety advantage to be derived from two engines, yet a lot of Twin Comanche accidents were related to the twin-engine nature of the airplane. The airplane was the lowest-cost twin available, so flight schools and users trading up from singles were attracted to it. But the safety potential was apparently negated in the first years of use as asymmetric thrust got the best of people in training as well as in bona fide engine-out situations. The people using the airplane and the FAA just did not approach the situation logically, and the Twin Comanche's strength became a weakness.

The training part of this is an example of how pilots should recognize that there are instances in which we can't bite the apple at all. In flying at slow speed on one engine, things might appear okay, not squirrelly, until the moment the airplane stalls. The entry into an asymmetric thrust-induced spin would be very quick; one second the pilot might be satisfied with the situation, the next second he might be in an extremely precarious predicament. If at low altitude, there would probably be no hope for recovery; if at a reasonable altitude, recovery would be possible only if proper action were to be taken very quickly.

The individual has to protect himself through avoidance of situations like that. Some highly proficient multiengine instructors were lost in accidents of this type, which is a good illustration of the fact that abstention is the *only* form of proficiency in some instances. I don't mind poking around on the tender spots of a twin, but give me more than a mile of altitude to use in case it wants to wrestle.

LANDING

The Twin Comanche has had another interesting experience that illustrates a further point. The airplane isn't one of the most satisfying in the world to land. It tends to hit level, regardless of a pilot's effort to make a tail-low landing, and ground contact is often with a very resounding thud. New and old Twin Comanche pilots shared the bad landings in the airplanes. I flew one for four years and never learned to make consistently good landings. And my definition of a good landing was one in which the tow bar was not jarred from its clip-type holder at the roof of the baggage compartment.

Despite the fact that the Twin Comanche was (and is) a bear to land, the airplane never had any abnormal landing accident history. Perhaps this suggests that an obvious characteristic, such as an open challenge to the pilot on every landing, might at times be less likely to cause real trouble than a conceptual area such as multiengine.

STRAPPED

The pilot's approach to handling qualities does not have a monopoly on determining safety potential. Hardware counts, too, and shoulder-harness systems in airplanes are highly individual items that can have a dramatic effect on aviation safety.

Like so many people, I rather shunned the use of harnesses for years. I'd leave them stowed (if the airplane was even equipped), and if the airplane was harnessless I never gave it a second thought. I suppose that the rationale was based on ego: I would protect myself against any potential sudden stop with a perfectly timed burst of brilliance. Then I was awakened from that dream by a flight surgeon at a safety meeting. He made the flat statement that 25 percent of the people who died in general aviation accidents would probably have survived if they had been wearing shoulder harnesses.

He was a man of more than words. There were also pictures, bloody awful pictures of corpses that were used to prove the point. I'll always remember one of a young pilot, a friend of a friend of mine, who looked in perfect shape except for a place on his head where contact was made with a windshield-mounted compass in a relatively minor accident. A shoulder harness would have prevented that.

I was sold. I was later to be further sold by a movie made by an airframe manufacturer. They crashed an airplane with two instrumented dummies aboard into a dirt bank at fifty knots in an experiment to test effectiveness of the restraint systems. The movie was a close-up of the cockpit at impact. One dummy had the shoulder harness on and probably survived. There was no question that the dummy without a harness was in much worse shape. Finally, the good experience with shoulder harnesses in agricultural aviation finished the sales job.

SPIN IN

Back to flying technique, where there are a lot of stall/spin accidents in which the individual clearly loads himself into the boat. Recently a couple of very experienced professional pilots flying a rather old two-place airplane provided a perfect illustration of this. Witnesses reported that the airplane zoomed up from behind the trees, stalled, and spun to the ground. Someone remarked that the pilot had been flying the little airplane like that since acquiring it and added that he'd been wondering when he would cash in. It finally happened, as was probably inevitable. Hopefully, the individual at least had enough sense to know that the fates were being sorely tempted, and in those last seconds he realized that the upcoming sudden stop was a creation of his own hand. When it was too late, it was too late. The deed was done, and the pilot's alleged skill or proficiency could in no way change the conclusion made inevitable by one sweeping stroke of bad judgment.

With such an accident in mind, the primary conclusion of any study of the relationship between the pilot and the airplane is that there is little mystery to general aviation accidents. They most frequently happen when a pilot pushes too far or attempts operation on the far side of individual ability, airplane performance, or structural limitations. And the total product of all this is applied to the number of hours flown to become the safety record.

HOW SAFE?

How is our safety record? How do we do when applied to the airplane in the real world?

For a benchmark, the crews of American Airlines once flew more than 6 million hours between fatal accidents. That is probably the best safety record in the history of public or private transportation, whether considered in terms of hours, passengers carried, or passenger miles operated. Compared with general aviation's rate of one fatal accident for every 45,000 hours of operation, the American Airlines record is nothing short of magnificent.

On an hourly basis, it is 133 times better; per mile, the figure would be even higher.

While general aviation in total doesn't do well by comparison with such a record, this in no way suggests that general aviation flying is inherently more dangerous than the flying done by American. No way. It is true that they do have performance advantages in their airplanes plus redundant systems and redundant crews, but general aviation also has some advantages. Our airplanes are simpler; if we do have a mishap it is at a slower speed with less aluminum to stop; and the majority of our operations are at airports where there is a tremendous margin built into the runway available. If they do have an equipment advantage, it is small—I'd arbitrarily say 5 or 10 percent. The real key to flying safely is in the way they operate their airplanes. The crews understand the risks, and they methodically fly in a manner that minimizes these risks. We can do the same thing. Flying any kind of airplane is just as safe as the pilot wants it to be.

Epilogue

In learning to fly, we accentuate the positive. We are learning to *do* something, to fly. In studying accidents, though, it is often obvious that the pilot might have erred more in the sense of doing something he shouldn't do rather than in the sense of doing something improperly. I thus thought that it would be worthwhile to offer a list of things *not* to do in an airplane. I do not offer this list as a course in how not to fly or as a complete list of things to avoid. Rather, it includes the most common items, based on accident reports, covering a great majority of the serious accidents. Feel free to add anything to it that you wish.

- Don't skimp on preflight duties. Check the weather and the airplane carefully.
- Don't fly VFR-day when the visibility is less than three miles and the ceiling is less than 1,000 feet

above the highest obstacle within five miles of the flight path.

- Don't fly VFR-night when the visibility is less than five miles and the ceiling is less than 2,000 feet above the highest obstacle within five miles of the flight path.
- Don't make any exceptions to the three prior rules and resolve to land at the nearest airport when any rule appears in danger of being compromised.
- Don't fail to check the weather when en route. Once every hour is a good practice.
- When IFR, don't leave the minimum descent altitude or the decision height until the runway is in sight. At night the rule is based on the runway lights. The approach lights do not count, day or night. They are to lead you to the runway, not to provide vertical guidance.
- Don't fly with a disregard for ice and thunderstorms. Given the right circumstances, either can easily prevail.
- Don't forget that you must fly the next mile before earning the right to fly the ones after it.
- Don't buzz or otherwise use an airplane as an outlet for exhibitionism.
- Don't fail to understand the importance of angle of attack and its relationship to the stall.
- Don't fail to recognize the possible need for reducing the angle of attack when considerable back pressure is being held on the wheel or stick during low-altitude maneuvers or when excessive aileron is being

held in the direction opposite the turn to prevent overbanking.

- Don't make downwind turns when speed or climb gradient is critical.
- Don't fail to ascertain that there is ample runway for a safe departure before every takeoff. This means careful calculations if there is any doubt.
- Don't hesitate to reduce the load when flying from small airports or in high-density altitude conditions.
- Don't overload an airplane under any circumstances, and check the center of gravity as within limits for every flight.
- Don't plan to land with less than one hour's fuel in the tanks.
- Don't forget that a midair collision can spoil your whole day. Look for, see, and avoid other traffic.
- Don't forget the principles of wake turbulence avoidance.
- Don't let anyone enter or leave your airplane when the engine is running.
- Don't forget to extend the landing gear of a retractable before each and every landing.
- Don't fail to get a good checkout in each make and model airplane flown.
- Don't explore any maneuvers that are not approved in the airplane being flown.
- Don't fly above 10,000 feet without supplementary oxygen.
- Don't fly when fatigued or ill.
- Don't fly when under the influence of alcohol or

drugs—either the direct or the lingering influence.

- Don't rely on anyone else for the successful completion of a flight. The pilot in command is solely responsible—in a practical, legal, and absolute sense.
- Don't fail to practice the things that can help you fly more safely.
- Don't fail to use a checklist for all operations. Do it all, every time.
- Don't fail to wear a shoulder harness.
- Don't ever base a "go" (or "keep going") decision on anything other than aeronautical factors. Business or personal considerations are secondary when flying.
- Don't ever fly with the thought *I think I can make it*. If you aren't sure, don't go.

Index